HIDDEN WORLDVIEWS

Eight Cultural Stories That Shape Our Lives

STEVE WILKENS
AND MARK L. SANFORD

IVP Academic

An imprint of InterVarsity Press
Downers Grove, Illinois

InterVarsity Press
P.O. Box 1400, Downers Grove, IL 60515-1426
ivpress.com
email@ivpress.com

InterVarsity Press® is the book-publishing division of InterVarsity Christian Fellowship/USA®, a movement of students and faculty active on campus at hundreds of universities, colleges and schools of nursing in the United States of America, and a member movement of the International Fellowship of Evangelical Students. For information about local and regional activities, visit intervarsity.org.

Design: Cindy Kiple

Cover images: ripped paper: Royce DeGrie/iStockphoto
            carnival masks: Images Etc. Ltd/Getty Images

Interior image: Birgitte Magnus/iStockphoto

ISBN 978-0-8308-3854-7

Printed in the United States of America ∞

Library of Congress Cataloging-in-Publication Data

Wilkens, Steve, 1955-
    Hidden worldviews: eight cultural stories that shape our lives/
    Steve Wilkens and Mark L. Sanford.
       p. cm.
    Includes bibliographical references.
    ISBN 0-978-8308-3854-7 (pbk.: alk. paper)
    1. Christianity—Philosophy. 2. Christianity and culture. 3.
    Ideology—Religious aspects—Christianity. I. Sanford, Mark L.,
    1951- II. Title.
    BR115.C8W543 2009
    261—dc22
                2009026581

| **P** | 26 | 25 | 24 | 23 | 22 | 21 | 20 | 19 | 18 | 17 | 16 | 15 | 14 | 13 | 12 | 11 | 10 | 9 |
| **Y** | 34 | 33 | 32 | 31 | 30 | 29 | 28 | 27 | 26 | 25 | 24 | 23 | 22 | 21 | 20 | 19 | 18 | 17 |

To my children,

Tiffany, Shawn and Katelyn,

who have taught me much about worldviews.

To Jack, Joe and Gene,

true brothers.

CONTENTS

ACKNOWLEDGMENTS

PROJECTS LIKE THIS ALWAYS GO WELL BEYOND the efforts of the authors, and we are deeply grateful for the contribution of those who have assisted us on a number of levels. We wish to thank Dr. Steve Green for developing and allowing us to modify and use his "transformational model" in the book. Mike Platter, my friend and pastor, provided a number of key insights on several chapters. Chris Adams, a friend and colleague at Azusa Pacific University, provided many helpful suggestions for the "Salvation by Therapy" chapter. Luis Montes supplied research assistance and offered thoughtful input on several chapters. Azusa Pacific University provided institutional support in the form of release time, research assistance, and writing retreats that created room for extended writing and reflection. Our manuscript was examined by three anonymous readers who offered very useful criticisms and guidance. Whoever you are, your incisive observations were accepted with gratitude, and we believe you have made an important contribution to the final product. With great appreciation we thank InterVarsity Press and our editor, Gary Deddo, for their support and patience in this process. Finally, we want to thank our students at Azusa Pacific University for their questions and input about worldviews. That dialogue has brought much clarity to the writing of this book.

1

WORLDVIEWS OVER COFFEE AT STARBUCKS

WHEN CHRISTIANS SEE A BOOK about worldviews, they automatically assume it is about apologetics—a defense of the Christian faith. That assumption is correct for this book as well, but this is apologetics with an important twist. Like other worldview books, we attempt to demonstrate the inadequacies of non-Christian thought systems or life orientations, and to convince readers that Christianity offers something better. But that is not our only goal, and perhaps it is not even our primary purpose. The twist is that this apologetics book also aims to provoke *Christians* to adopt a Christian worldview. Too often, we assume that non-Christian worldviews stay safely on the other side of the church door. As you will see below, we believe that this is far from the case. In fact, much of this book grows out of our own self-reflection to isolate areas where hidden worldviews, alien to Christianity, have crept into our thoughts and lifestyles.

The theory that Christians are largely immune to the influence of non-Christian thought structures is often unconsciously perpetuated by worldview books that identify atheistic existentialism, postmodern deconstructionism, Marxism or similar philosophical systems as Christianity's main competitors. These worldviews are, to be sure, contrary to a Christian view of the world in fundamental ways, and it is completely proper to frame an intellectual response to them. However, stopping here has two important limitations. First, somewhere along the line, Christians have bought into the idea that philosophies born and perpetuated in universities represent the greatest challenge to a Christian worldview. We believe that is wrong-headed. How many people do you know who are locked in deep conflict over whether to become an atheistic existentialist or a Christian? How many committed Marxists do you run into on a daily basis? The reality is that we don't really encounter massive herds of people enticed by the thought systems found in a typical worldview book.

The second limitation of most worldview books is that they let Christian readers off the hook too easily. After reading such books, they frequently will conclude that the author is correct about the deficiencies of competing ideas and the sufficiency of Christian ideas. Because of this agreement, Christians often further conclude that their faith remains untainted by contrary worldviews. This creates a dangerous situation if the real competition for the hearts and minds of Christians and non-Christians alike does not spring from the academy, where the worldviews are clearly formulated and expressed. What if the real competition comes from worldviews we do not see at all, even if they surround us?

We believe this is the situation. It is not the worldviews that begin as theories or intellectual systems that mold the lives and beliefs of most people. Instead, the most powerful influences come from worldviews that emerge from culture. They are all around us, but are so deeply embedded in culture that we don't see them. In other words, these worldviews are hidden in plain sight. We will occasionally call them "lived worldviews" because we are more likely to absorb them through cultural contact than adopt them through a rational evaluation of competing theories. These lived worldviews are popular philosophies of life that have few intellectual proponents but vast numbers of practitioners.

The eight belief systems we identify as hidden worldviews—individualism, consumerism, nationalism, moral relativism, naturalism, the New Age, postmodern tribalism and salvation by therapy—fit this model. This is certainly not an exhaustive list,[1] but they are among the most pervasive life-shaping perspectives in North American culture. If you observe carefully, you hear and see them everywhere—in offices, dormitories, Internet chat rooms and over-coffee-at-Starbucks conversations. Moreover, they are not limited to secular venues. Because of their stealthy nature, these worldviews find their way behind the church doors, mixed in with Christian ideas and sometimes identified as Christian positions.

This accounts for the "apologetic twist" mentioned at the beginning of the book. Many Christians have imported chunks of these worldviews without being aware of it. This is difficult to avoid because they are embedded throughout North American culture. Moreover, because we do not encounter them as intellectual systems, they usually fly under the radar of conscious thought. Thus, their power over us is increased since we are often unaware of how they shape our life and ideas. In short, no one is immune from the influence of these perspectives. They are very real competitors with Christianity, and they stake their claim on the lives of Christians and nonbelievers alike.

Because we will examine worldviews that are absorbed through culture rather than adopted through rational appraisal, the structure and approach of this book will differ from many others in the "worldview" category. Most worldview books proceed by investigating the writings of those who propose intellectual thought systems, and then they undertake a thorough evaluation of the coherence of these ideas. This makes perfect sense when examining worldviews that originate as theoretical systems. However, the over-coffee-at-Starbucks worldviews we examine do not have this sort of starting point. They may indeed have philosophical and academic connections or origins, but by the

---

[1]You might note, for example, that we do not address the major world religions, which certainly fit the category of lived worldviews. We have not examined these for two reasons. First, we want to focus on the North American cultural context, and even though the influence of other religions is growing here, we do not believe their impact is as direct as those we have selected. Second, addressing this area in an adequate manner would double the length of this book.

time these ideas trickle down to popular American culture, they manifest themselves in different ways. For example, what we call postmodern tribalism has roots in postmodern philosophy, as the name implies, but it is not the same as postmodern philosophy. Capitalist economic theory has influenced both consumerism and individualism, two worldviews examined later in this book. It is a mistake, however, to equate either with capitalism or, for that matter, to assume that capitalism is the only influence on these systems. Thus, we will examine worldviews in their everyday expression, not their more purified theoretical forms, because that is how most people experience them and are drawn under their influence. (This also, by the way, cuts down significantly on the number of footnotes.)

Our second departure from the traditional model is to approach worldviews as more than just intellectual systems. Some readers will take us to task for this because they define *worldview* as an intentional attempt to frame answers to the deepest questions in life. Such attempts consciously begin with the aim of directly addressing questions about God, reality, knowledge, goodness, human nature and other foundational questions. Most of the lived worldviews we will examine do not start here. Nevertheless, as we will see, they imply answers to all of the questions that theoretical worldviews attempt to address. Moreover, the effect of our lived worldviews is the same sought by their theoretical cousins. They tell us what we should love or despise, what is valuable or unimportant, and what is good or evil. All worldviews offer definitions of the fundamental human problem and how we might fix it. When you get right down to it, every worldview attempts to answer the question "What must we do to be saved?" Regardless of whether it comes to us as a theoretical construct or is soaked up by osmosis from culture, our worldview will have a deep impact on how we view our universe, ourselves and our actions.

Because these hidden worldviews do what theoretical worldviews do (propose answers to fundamental questions and shape our lives), we do not hesitate to use the term *worldview* to describe the systems in this book. While we do not reject the validity of the intentional, rational examination of these questions, we think it stops too soon. The reality of life is that, while humans are rational beings, we are not *just* rational beings. The vast majority of us do not commit to a worldview by initiating a purely intellectual comparison of competing philosophies and choosing what appears to be the most coherent one. We don't just think our way into worldviews, we *experience* them.

For most of us, our worldviews come to us more like a story or faith commitment rather than a system of ideas we select among a buffet of intellectual options. It is certainly the case that we are able to extract ideas that characterize each worldview, and this will occupy a significant amount of our attention in each chapter. Nevertheless, we want to be aware that, for most of us, worldviews are not primarily systems of interlinked ideas and beliefs, but they are experienced, absorbed and expressed in the midst of life.

REAL-LIFE, WHOLE-LIFE WORLDVIEWS

If what we have said so far makes sense, it means that the entire worldview enterprise is a lot messier than is often implied by many books on the topic. James Sire's understanding of worldview helps illuminate some reasons behind this messiness. As he defines it, "A worldview is a commitment, a fundamental orientation of the heart, that can be expressed as a story or in a set of presuppositions (assumptions which may be true, partially true or entirely false) which we hold (consciously or subconsciously, consistently or inconsistently) about the basic constitution of reality, and that provides the foundation on which we live and move and have our being."[2] We will break Sire's definition down into pieces slowly, but it is important from the beginning to clarify what he means by *heart*. Our culture tends to speak of the heart in reference to feelings or emotions. Sire reminds us, however, that the biblical concept of heart is much richer than this. It includes the emotions, but also encompasses wisdom, desire and will, spirituality and intellect. In short, the heart is, "the central defining element of the human person."[3]

---

[2]James Sire, *Naming the Elephant: Worldview as a Concept* (Downers Grove, Ill.: InterVarsity Press, 2004), p. 122.
[3]Ibid., p. 124.

Equating *heart* with the entire person helps us identify one important factor that contributes to real-life worldview messiness. Worldviews are not just cognitive constructs in which the relative amounts of truth and error included in them determine the relative success or failure of our lives. Real human beings, beings with "heart," are multidimensional; our lives possess physical, economic, psychological, political, spiritual, social and intellectual facets. This is why we intuitively recognize that a person with a clear and coherent grasp of intellectual truth still lives a less than complete life if they are economically careless or a psychological basket case (or, we would add, spiritually indifferent). To isolate the intellectual component as the exclusive concern of worldview formation, as many worldview books do, is reductionistic. It condenses a real multidimensional person to a single aspect of his or her actual existence. To be sure, our intellect is important, but if taken in isolation it fails to put complete and real people in the picture.

The charge of reductionism is one you will hear frequently throughout the following chapters because the strength of each worldview we examine also turns out to be its "Achilles' heel" when that insight is absolutized. Consumerism, for example, correctly reminds us that we are finite beings who perish unless we consume at least some of our environment's resources. Consumerism's big mistake, however, is that it defines us solely as physical, consuming beings. Stated otherwise, consumerism is a reductionistic worldview because it absolutizes our physical and economic dimensions and gives insufficient attention to remaining aspects of human existence. Other worldviews, in turn, absolutize some other facet of our experience to the exclusion of others.

As you may anticipate, then, part of our argument is that Christianity avoids and corrects the reductionisms of these competing systems and offers a full-orbed account of human life. Thus, we will find much that we can consent to and learn from within non-Christian worldviews. At the same time, we maintain that any perspective that fails to do justice to every God-created dimension of human life cannot be described as a Christian worldview. To put it in the language of Sire's definition, if "heart" refers to the whole person, we must pursue a wholehearted worldview that avoids reductionism.

WORLDVIEWS AS STORY

If Sire's definition of worldview as a "heart orientation," a set of commitments that encompasses the entire person, reveals one factor that clutters up our task, his suggestion that worldviews can be told as a story discloses a second messy element in our approach. The usual mode of operation in worldview books is to compare and evaluate propositional systems, which because they are systems, are neat and orderly. Stories, on the other hand, are not quite as tidy. However, we believe that the concept of story as a metaphor for worldview is more true-to-life than a recital of propositions that one believes to be true, for two reasons.

The first reason we prefer the concept of worldview as story is that we believe that our knowledge of God is revealed in a manner that is more analogous to a narrative than a set of propositions. It doesn't take a deep investigation of Scripture to discover that it is not written as a logically constructed, tightly interconnected and cross-referenced system of truthful propositions. We may certainly be able to distill from the Bible such a system, but it does not come packaged in that way. Instead, as we will develop in chapter ten, Scripture's overall structure resembles an epic story stretching from creation to history's consummation, encompassing smaller stories of God's interaction with people over a broad span of years and cultural contexts. This bigger narrative of God's involvement with us, what we will call "God's story," provides the foundation on which we attempt to discern a Christian worldview and the broad horizon against which we all live our individual lives (or stories).

Second, in addition to God's revelation coming in a manner similar to story, our worldviews unfold in a storylike manner. Consider how we come to know others. We do not discover who someone really is by asking for a set of propositions they assent to, although this may play a part. Instead, we gain insight into a person's identity by learning where they come from, key life experiences, what they love, what sorts of relationships they have and a multitude of other storylike features. While we may talk about these matters in propositional terms, even these propositions are products of our experiences. Thus, while propositional beliefs are an essential aspect of worldview examination, these spring from the messy process that we will call "our story."

OUR STORY AND WORLDVIEW FORMATION

At birth, we arrive in a world filled with competing visions of purpose, truth and goodness, and we experience them in a multitude of ways. Worldviews come at us, not as fully-formed systems of interrelated ideas, but in bits and pieces. We encounter them through national heritage, religion, family influence, the educational system, peer groups, various media and countless additional sources. They are transmitted by these sources through such diverse forms as music, political speeches, advertising, unsolicited advice from friends or family and, yes, via our coffee-at-Starbucks conversations. And sometimes what is not said explicitly in these different modes of communication shapes our worldviews as much as what is said. In short, these influences are so pervasive throughout culture that we may not even see them at all.

Moreover, worldview formation, like a story, is not a static affair. Every good narrative, including our own, has a dynamic quality. Like stories, lives have a beginning, a middle and an ending that include specific contexts, unique characters, plot twists, conflicts or crises, along with resolutions that set up the next episode. As a result, even when the fundamental outlines of our worldview hold up over a lifetime, the details go through modifications based on our psychological development, new events or relationships, exposure to new ideas or a number of other factors.

As the story unfolds, however, the sequence, actors and plot development are only the most visible features. In reality, our stories are structured, in large part, by forces that reside beneath the surface. My actions manifest the subterranean influence of my self-understanding, my convictions and my values. Things that happen to me and around me, many of them beyond my immediate control, provide the setting for my story. Nevertheless, what occurs in the various chapters, what my character becomes, is also molded by what I believe and value. Thus, in the following diagram we will trace the components of our story, our worldview, as they radiate from our interior stories toward external expression and action.

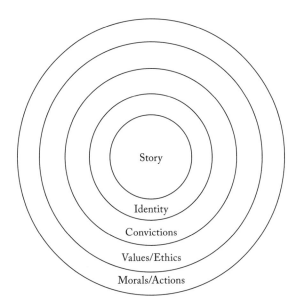

Story:	The central narrative of our life
Identity:	How we see ourselves and present ourselves to others
Convictions:	Those beliefs that make up how reality works for us
Values/Ethics:	What we believe we should do and what we take to be our highest priorities
Morals/Actions:	The realm of doing that includes all of our activities

Figure 1. Transformation model (developed by Dr. Steve Green)

Story: Moving Toward Action

In the opening scene of *Fiddler on the Roof,* Tevye says that, because of tradition, "everyone knows who he is." That is what our story does; it gives us an identity. The identity level of our being encompasses such things as our concept of success or where we believe we fit into the scheme of things. In the myriad of relationships—with God, myself, others and the physical world—my story provides an interpretive grid that expresses the importance and value of the various "others" I encounter. If my identity is invested in financial well-being rather than in friendships, I may not think twice about a long-distance relocation when offered the dream job with a fat raise, even if it means leaving long-term friendships. However, if my identity has been closely connected with my job status and financial well-being for some time, it is unlikely that I will have many real friendships to consider when the job offer comes. The definition of success within a consumerist worldview will be much different from someone whose story emphasizes enduring relationships.

Closely intertwined with our identity is what we call our convictions. Our convictions might be viewed as a distillation of our story as it is filtered through our sense of identity into a system of propositions that forms the ideological framework for our story. These convictions play a central role in our story because we believe them to be true descriptions of what Sire's definition refers to as "the basic constitution of reality." They express our ideas about what the whole world is like, how it works, the means by which we understand it properly, and what its purpose is.

These convictions are vital because they describe how we understand and interpret the world. It is the means by which we articulate our worldview. We can illustrate this by contrasting the convictions of a scientific naturalist with a Christian theist. As we will see below, scientific naturalism's central convictions argue that the world is a closed system, containing nothing more than physical components whose interactions are determined by ironclad, absolute laws. This rules out the existence of any nonphysical reality, God included. By contrast, the Christian theist views the world as open to the activity of God. For the theist, then, the laws that govern nature originate from God and provide an accurate description of physical interactions within creation. However, since these laws are creations of God, they are not absolute. Realities exist that transcend such laws.

Thus, the stories behind a naturalist's and a theist's convictions differ radically. Both may see the same facts, but the convictions that shape their respective interpretations of these facts are quite different. In fact, it is not an overstatement to say that a naturalist and a theist could live in the same house and, at the same time, inhabit two entirely different universes. What exists (and does not exist) in my universe, the means by which it is known most accurately, my place in this universe, and a host of other questions will have answers that are molded by my convictions. If I change my convictions, my world, at least as I experience it, changes with them.

Convictional beliefs about the nature of reality and how that reality is known radiate outward to shape our ethics (what we believe we should or should not do) and values (what we take to be priorities). What is the good or right way to live? Which moral principles, if any, are nonnegotiable? Which are relative or conditional? Which values should mark the priorities that shape who we are and how we use our time? To illustrate, we frequently say that we do not have enough time for something. In reality, these statements are rarely true. If we are honest, "not enough time" can almost always be translated as, "I did not do that because it was not a high priority." Someone committed to an individualistic worldview will find time for different things than we would see on a New Ager's schedule. Similarly, the highest ethical loyalties of a nationalist will vary significantly from those of a committed Christian.

Finally, our ethics shapes our actions. This is the realm of doing that includes activities from our voting patterns to our use of money to the time we spend with family, and everything in between. This is the part of our stories that is most evident to those around us, and it is certainly how most people start to learn what we think of ourselves, what ethical principles we embrace, and what convictions govern our lives. In short, our behaviors are the stage on which we play out our stories.

Now that we have reached the outer layer of our stories, two things should become evident as we think about the relationship between our actions, which form the more public facet of our lives, and the interior, more private aspects of our stories. The first was hinted at above; our actions do not exist in a vacuum, disconnected from other aspects of life. There is, as the saying goes, much more to us than meets the eye. Second, it seems clear that our visible actions are not always consistent with those other parts of our lives that don't "meet the eye." What I do is not always congruent with what I believe. In fact, an important premise of this book is that what we believe, *really* believe, is not always congruent with what we say we believe or think we want to believe. One can, for example, profess Christianity and live like an individualist. We probably ought to fix that, and a careful evaluation of our worldview can be an important part of that fix.

A CONGRUENT STORY

Several years ago a fascinating story hit the news about a seventy-three-year-old Catholic woman, Eleanor Boyer, who had won the New Jersey State lottery. After federal and state taxes were deducted, she had over eight million dollars left. We don't know your financial situation, but this is a sum sufficient to capture our attention. So is the amount of money this woman gave away. In fact, she gave it all away—to her church and to organizations in her town that helped people in need. When the reporter asked her why she donated all the winnings, her response was "God takes care of me."

If we would paste our own picture into this story, we quickly recognize how difficult it is to bring congruity to our worldview. Many people are quick to say that God will provide for their needs or that it would be wrong to spend money extravagantly when it could provide life-saving relief to people in dire need. Yet our actions, if we would receive an unexpected, after-tax eight-million-dollar windfall, may not have as much congruency with statements made about our convictions before we hit the jackpot as those of the woman above. This example, and millions of others we could create, reminds us of the vast difference between what we call *confessional* beliefs, ideas that remain exclusively on the intellectual level, and *convictional* beliefs, beliefs that are reflected in our actions.

Careful worldview examination requires that we constantly hold up our convictions against the mirror of our actions to see where our confessional beliefs are incongruous with our convictional beliefs. Christians often find it much easier to talk a good game by reciting the right creeds and embracing the proper doctrinal statements than to actually live by the principles embodied in them. But Christians are not the only people susceptible to incongruity (or hypocrisy, if you prefer that word). In extreme circumstances, scientific naturalists may find themselves in prayer to God. A moral relativist may live as if universal moral standards do exist. Regardless of one's worldview, it is important to integrate what we say we believe and what we actually do. This is not possible unless we live reflectively, carefully examining both our ideas and actions to see if they are in sync. That is, then, one of our main tasks in this book.

A second reason to subject various worldviews to rigorous examination brings us back to the more traditional apologetic task of contrasting a Christian worldview with competing ideas. Christians will agree that it is often difficult to live a life that is consistent with our convictions. At the same time, they should also agree that (1) the central convictions of a Christian worldview are consistent with each other and (2) acting in accordance with Christian convictions yields good results in our lives. We don't believe that either is the case with the competing worldviews we examine in this book. For example, a bedrock belief for moral relativism is that no universally valid moral principles exist. However, a second relativist conviction is that we should be tolerant of those whose moral views differ from ours. The glaring contradiction here is that the demand of tolerance by all and for all is a moral standard that is inconsistent with the relativist's claim that no universal moral standards exist. This is certainly in tension with (1) above, which argues that a worldview should be internally consistent.

Moral relativism also runs afoul of (2), which says that living out one's worldview should lead to beneficial results. We will argue that moral relativists really don't live out the first conviction (no universal moral principles exist), and it is a good thing they don't. The logical outcome of this conviction is dog-eat-dog chaos, not exactly the type of beneficial result we look for in a good worldview. In sum, then, we encourage reflection on a series of worldviews because it can reveal their logical or practical flaws, and hopefully help us avoid them.

Our third reason for vigilance about worldview incongruities is specific to our task of helping Christians develop a Christian worldview. Without reflection, ideas contrary to a Christian worldview creep into our convictional beliefs, and we might not even realize it. The problem here is that, while confessional beliefs exist on the conscious level (which must be the case if we "confess" them), many of our convictional beliefs work on the subconscious level, as Sire's worldview definition reminds us. We may not be aware of what our true convictions are, but that does not make them less real or determinative for our lives. Thus, a careful examination of postmodern tribalism, for example, might reveal areas where Christians have allowed un-Christian ideas about race, gender or national superiority to infiltrate their worldview. Or, as illustrated above, considering how we might handle an unforeseen cash windfall might show us that, despite our claims to worship God alone, we have become mammon-worshiping consumerists. Therefore, Christians need to learn what these competing stories say. In doing so, we can discover how our convictions have been shaped by worldviews that are incompatible with what we want to believe. Without careful, conscious reflection, our Christian story can easily be hijacked by alien stories that take our lives in directions we don't want to go. Because what we are not conscious of *can* hurt us, it is important to take an inventory of our true convictions.

Each of the worldviews in this book is part of the cultural air we breathe. Moreover, each of these worldviews has the power to distort our Christian story, a power that grows in proportion to our lack of awareness of its influence. Paul reminds us of this in Romans 12:2 when he states, "Do not conform any longer to the pattern of this world." *Aion*, the word translated as "world," is more literally translated "age." The "pattern of this age" refers to the dominant ways of thinking, the stories, that shape the world around us. Paul is not, therefore, talking about avoiding any particular kind of activities. He warns us against a deeper, more pervasive danger, the danger of conforming to a story that differs from God's story for us.

TRANSFORMATION TO GOD'S STORY

Paul's antidote to conformity to the "patterns of this age" is found in the last part of the verse: "but be transformed by the renewing of your mind. Then you will be able to test and approve what God's will is—his good, pleasing and perfect will." Instead of conforming to the stories of our age, Paul says that we need to be transformed to God's story, God's "good, pleasing and perfect will." This raises a point that is too often forgotten. The worldview of a Christian, if it is to remain a Christian worldview, needs to be set within God's story.

Paul clearly indicates that the kind of transformation that aligns us with God's story has to impact our minds. By this, however, he is not just speaking of a collection of confessional beliefs. As we have seen, what we claim to believe does not always transform our lives. Instead, the renewal of our minds envisions a transformation of our whole beings—our intellects, wills, desires, relationships and spirituality (and thus encompasses what Sire earlier refers to as "heart"). Paul's call for a renewal of the mind stands in contrast to most Christian preaching and teaching, which is focused on changing the outermost circle of our story—the behavioral level. While the actions of the Christian should undergo a transformative process, changing behaviors alone is not transformation. It attacks the symptoms rather than the disease. In the end, behavioral change is a pale counterfeit of a whole-person transformation that works from the mind outward.

Transformation that does not involve the mind comes at a high cost. Steve Garber's book *The Fabric of Faithfulness* asked a probing question: "Why do some Christians leave college, and five to ten years later they have also left Christianity? Why do other Christians complete college and continue to integrate their Christian faith with a new set of life circumstances?" His findings were fascinating. Without exception, those who successfully integrated faith with life followed three practices. They developed a relationship with a mentor who practiced an active Christian life. Second, they met regularly with peers who were deeply committed to living out their Christianity. Finally, they had developed a Christian worldview sufficient to meet the challenges of the competing worldviews they encountered after leaving college.

Our book's eye is obviously focused on the third critical element that Garber identifies. When our minds do not undergo continuing transformation through reflection on our entire life, our stories inevitably deviate from God's plotline. However, development of a Christian worldview sufficient to meet the challenges of the competing worldviews is not unrelated to the first two factors noted by Garber. Our relationships frame the context of our stories, and it is within the accountability of such relationships that we align our stories to God's story. Our examination of life should not just be an individual endeavor but needs to occur within the context of a community. In fact, this book itself was birthed out of discussions on these matters within adult Bible classes and university discipleship groups. Without all three elements—mentoring, reflective fellowship and worldview formation—the ever-present non-Christian worldviews begin to work their corrosive effects on our lives.

In the following chapters, we will examine eight stories, widespread within American culture, that compete with a Christian worldview. They are, to some extent, artificial constructions; probably no person alive exemplifies any of these types in a pure form. These influences, as we have said, come at us in fragments from multiple directions, and most real lives are a composite of these forces. Christians are not exempt from this, and this premise stands at the heart of this book. Our worldview, if we live an unexamined life, can be adulterated by hidden elements that dilute and corrupt it.

As we evaluate these competing stories, we will focus heavily on the characteristic convictions of each worldview. This intellectual component is necessary because, as we have seen above, our convictions play a central role in our worldviews. However, it will be important to remember that the stakes are much higher than simply a contest about which ideology comes out the winner. Worldviews are ultimately about full-orbed, multidimensional, real human lives, and how we can get the most from them. In short, as we will say often in the following chapters, all worldviews are ultimately about salvation, even if they don't use that vocabulary.

The Christian worldview places an extremely high value on life, which is the reason it is so deeply interested in salvation. If life is valuable, it makes sense to examine the stories that shape our lives to make certain we experience the abundance God desires for them. To this end, we will close the book with two chapters about Christian worldviews. The first (chapter ten) outlines the contours of a Christian worldview in a narrative form and explores places where it differs from the others examined in this text. Our final chapter (chapter eleven) explores the question of how one develops and nurtures a real-life, whole-life worldview.

2

INDIVIDUALISM

I Am the Center of the Universe

SOMETIMES IT IS HELPFUL TO DEFINE something by first stating what it is not. When we talk about individualism in this chapter, we are not referring to a healthy and biblical belief in the inherent dignity and sacredness of each person. Nor are we talking about a vital diversity of personal interests and abilities. Instead, individualism, as used in this chapter, is the belief that the individual is the primary reality and that our understanding of the universe and lifestyle should be centered in oneself. Individualism says that my unique interests and goals should be pursued, as much as possible, by whatever means deemed proper. Thus, individuals strive for autonomy and self-sufficiency, relying on others only as they contribute to one's personal pursuits. Family, community and society are, at best, secondary considerations.

If this brief description of individualism sounds familiar, it should not come as a shock. Individualism has been deeply ingrained in American culture from its beginning. Whether it is the penniless immigrant who becomes a self-made millionaire, the solitary cowboy riding out of Dodge City or the starving artist who defies convention, our folklore celebrates the individual who creates his or her own unique path. Thus, like the other lived worldviews in this book, individualism does not really find its origins in an intellectual system, but as a type of story about who we should be.

Perhaps the best analysis of American individualism today is found in the book *Habits of the Heart* written by Robert Bellah and his colleagues. *Habits* refers to two distinct types of individualism, both common in American culture. The first form is "utilitarian individualism." Utilitarian individualism has been a dominant force in America since its founding and has often fueled the quest for the "American Dream." This version of individualism focuses on personal achievement and material success, and believes that the social good automatically follows from the individual pursuit of one's own interests. Thus, the utilitarian individualism does not necessarily reject the structures and rules of society. Instead, they are viewed primarily as guidelines or tools that help the individual work efficiently within the system. In other words, there is a willingness to accept certain restrictions on personal behavior, such as laws prohibiting bribery, because a system that requires honest business dealings ultimately benefits those who work hard.

The second form Bellah identifies, "expressive individualism," is a reaction to the limitations of utilitarian individualism. While the latter generally advises that we pursue individual success by conformity to the rules and common practices of society, *expressive* individualism worships the freedom to express our uniqueness against constraints and conventions. Because rules and social conventions encourage conformity, they are viewed as a threat to personal expression and individuality. The danger is that we will be absorbed into the herd. Thus, liberation and fulfillment are central themes in expressive individualism and find articulation in statements like "I need to be free to be me." Freedom becomes the rationale for reducing any responsibilities perceived as limitations to my personal autonomy or fulfillment, whether those responsibilities are social, moral, religious or family duties. Where utilitarian individualism sees our social systems as a means for attaining our individual goals, expressive individualism generally views these systems as obstacles to individual freedom.

What makes individualism such a temptation to Christians is that this philosophy, as noted above, is woven into our cultural fabric. Individualism's influence on Christians is apparent in the often-heard statements like, "My faith is between God and me," "My religion is a personal thing," or "I believe in God. I don't need to go to church." While Christianity embraces the truth that God is interested and involved in each of our lives, individualism takes this to such an extreme that it ceases to be Christian truth. In this chapter, we will take a closer look at the convictional beliefs behind individualism, the truths in this worldview and the perversions that make individualism so attractive.

I AM THE PRIMARY REALITY IN THE UNIVERSE

At the heart of individualism lies the belief that each individual person constitutes the center of one's universe. At first glance, this seems to be a view that most people would not openly embrace. We are, after all, frequently told to look out for and care about others. Moreover, no one really likes a person who is obviously self-centered. However, we all have to admit that the tug toward a self-centered life is strong, and this tempts us to cloak selfish intentions by using the language of unselfishness. If we are honest, we will admit that many things we claim to do sacrificially or just because they are right are exactly the same actions that bring us personal benefit. With a bit of unbiased examination of our motives, it is hard to deny that we have a strong bias toward our individual interests. Thus, despite what we may say to the contrary, it is not hard to make the case that we are more self-centered than we are willing to admit.

If moral and religious teachings are full of warnings against placing our individual self at the center of the universe, why is it so ingrained into our culture? It would be easy just to say that it is part of our sinful nature, and this is a big part of the answer. However, it is also clear that earlier ages (which I doubt were any less sinful than our own) have been much less individualistic in character. In the ancient or medieval world, one became a hero by submission and conformity. So why are ideas like submission and conformity to authority viewed in such a negative light today? We believe that a large part of the individualistic impulse today comes out of a sense of profound disappointment with corporate institutions. Whether we are talking about churches, governments or financial corporations, history reveals that institutions are subject to deep corruption and have often badly abused the very people they were supposed to protect and nurture.

A short answer to the question of individualism's roots then, is that it can be seen as a defensive action. The utilitarian individualist usually views a church, government or corporation as a necessary evil. These organizations cannot be always counted on to protect my interests, so the goals of these corporate bodies should never claim my first loyalty. Instead, they are useful only as a means to achieving my personal goals.

Expressive individualism, on the other hand, views corporate entities as more evil than necessary. It fears that demands for conformity from these institutions drain the life from us. This form of individualism, then, is characterized by rebellion against mass culture as a way of protecting one's identity. In either case, individualism is an attempt to guard ourselves against the threats presented by social and religious institutions. If we cannot control these institutions to make them work for our interests, we retrench by finding our primary reality in something we can control to a greater degree: our own life and interests. In other words, we make our self the primary reality of the universe.

MY END JUSTIFIES MY MEANS

The Greek city-state had an interesting way of calling citizens together when a vote for some type of action was needed. If, for example, another city-state was marching against them to do battle, a person would walk the streets blowing a horn, announcing that all should gather in the amphitheater just outside of town. When the citizens of the city heard this, they would close up their shops, head to the amphitheater to get the news and fulfill their civic duty by voicing their response. However, some shop-owners refused to shut down, hoping to do extra business while the competitors' businesses were closed. The Greeks referred to such persons as *idiotes*, which means someone is closed up in their own world who, concerned only with personal goals, ignores the greater good.

Individualism generates a world full of *idiotes*, and the reason is obvious. If I view myself as the primary reality within the universe, this determines *how* I do things. When I picture myself as the central reality, my goals have greater significance than those of any other person or group. It follows, then, that the most direct route to my specific goals will be the best one. If my primary goals are better achieved by ignoring the needs of society and making a quick buck, my shop stays open. To outline this principle in broader terms, individualism naturally gravitates toward the idea that the end justifies the means, or perhaps more accurately, *my* end justifies *my* means. This is not a new belief, but in our culture it finds a ready ally in utilitarian individualism. Whenever success at any endeavor is a highly valued goal, this rationale justifies behaviors that others find questionable (since it does not serve their needs). However, if this behavior results in my success, and if my success, in whatever way I define it, is my primary aim, then it is the right choice.

The idea that my ends justify my means finds a natural connection to expressive individualism as well. Several of us had gathered at the beach in Southern California to enjoy the sun, water and each other. As I was walking back from the restroom to our section of the beach, I passed some twentysomething adults playing volleyball together. I heard one woman say, "I would much rather be perceived as a liar than as a loser." She said it all. When we want others to think of us as a winner and believe that lying will get us there, we can put a pretty steep discount on the value of truth, not to mention the people who expect to hear truth from us. Thus, individualism leads to a rather astonishing conclusion. If one cannot tell the truth without being perceived as a loser, we have an obligation to lie (assuming it is not our goal to be seen as a loser).

I Am My Own Moral Conscience

As implied above, if my goals determine the means by which I will pursue them, it will be a natural step to extend this into the realm of ethics. After all, my goals determine what I find valuable. Therefore, if my goals differ from those others strive for and I am more in tune than anyone else about my goals, I am the one best positioned to understand the values that will get me there. Moreover, since my goals are unique, I should expect that my values also will be unique to me. From here, it is a short step to the conclusion that I am in a better position to judge how well I conform to my values than anyone else. In other words, if I am the center of my reality and know that reality better than anyone else, a corollary belief is that others have no right to criticize how I live. How can anyone tell others how they should live their lives?

When individualists reject the right of others to question their moral actions, this is often viewed as an attempt to evade personal responsibility, and no doubt this is frequently the case. However, if we properly understand individualism, the real question is not whether I have a moral responsibility, but who or what is the authority behind my moral responsibility. If individualism is correct, it becomes irresponsible for me to allow others to impose their moral beliefs and standards on me since, as stated above, others lack direct knowledge about my aims and values. It would be like judging a work of poetry by the rules of mathematics. Thus, individualism dictates that I become the authoritative source of what is right and wrong for me.

FREEDOM AND FULFILLMENT ARE MY RIGHT

Some years back, Dennis Rodman, then with the Chicago Bulls, made derogatory comments about Mormons during a series with the Utah Jazz. These statements drew much criticism from Utah's Mormon population and a fine from the commissioner of the NBA. In an interview, a sportscaster asked Mr. Rodman if he accepted responsibility for his actions. Mr. Rodman's response was, "I thought we lived in a country where we were free do whatever we wanted as long as we did not kill someone." The idea that we are free to do or say anything short of murder probably pushes the principle of freedom beyond the comfort level for most of us, but it is an extreme form of a view that we have become accustomed to. If fulfillment is my right (a logical conclusion of the belief that we stand at the center of the universe) and the sensibilities, rules or traditions of others stand in the way of my pursuit of fulfillment, I need to be free of these limitations.

While most worldviews acknowledge the right of individuals to act freely to some degree, it is interesting to note what happens to values when freedom fights its way to the top of the virtue hierarchy. In classical thought, the four cardinal (or basic) virtues were identified as prudence, courage, moderation and justice. The idea was that a person became free when she lived according to such virtues. In other words, the limitations to our freedom were viewed as internal, moral obstacles that could be overcome by developing and internalizing these virtuous characteristics.

When freedom becomes the cardinal virtue, it radically redefines the traditional virtues listed above. If my individual goals are primary, justice can no longer be a principle in which the obligations and rights of two parties are viewed equally. Individualism puts me at the center of the universe and does not allow me to consider "the other" as an equal. Second, when individual liberty is our primary value, we identify obstacles to fulfillment as something outside us (e.g., other people, mass culture, government restrictions) rather than internal deficiencies in our character. In other words, goodness is not obtained by internal transformation, but by rearrangement of external circumstances. Finally, and related to the last point, traditional virtues such as courage are no longer desirable characteristics because they represent restrictions to our freedom. When we are told that we should be courageous, this assumes that external standards should shape our actions and limit our freedom. However, if freedom is our highest value, courage (and all the other classical virtues) becomes a hindrance if it conflicts with my idea of fulfillment.

PERFORMANCE DEFINES OUR VALUE

Individualism's assertion that the end justifies the means leads inevitably to the question of how we determine what our ends are. If each person is the center of his or her universe, the value of one's universe then depends on one's individual value. In short, if I don't amount to much, then my universe doesn't count for much either. My performance defines my self-worth. What we do and what we accomplish is equated with who we are.

The idea that our value is measured by our accomplishments can be seen in our idea of the hero. The next time you walk through the aisles of your local video store, take a stroll through the action section. You will immediately notice that this category is dominated by the solitary hero who saves the person, community, nation or, in the case of James Bond, the whole world. In these movies, hundreds of people may be blown up, shot, abducted by evil aliens or sucked dry by thirsty vampires, but they don't count for much. Our attention is riveted on the extraordinary individual who saves the day, because saving the day is what makes one worthwhile.

In its better moments, our stories acknowledge that even solitary heroes need the help of others. Those who save the universe usually have a sidekick or partner, although they are often more of an obstacle than any real help. Yet we envision ourselves as the hero in these movies, not the bumbling sidekick. In utilitarian individualism, everyday heroism involves excelling or standing out within existing social structures (e.g., workplace, academia, athletics). For expressive individualism, heroism is often calculated in terms of the distance a person creates between their performance and the social structures. Thus, for example, an artist is rarely rewarded by creating pieces that appeal to the masses. In whatever form the solitary hero appears, it is difficult to ignore the cultural impact of the idea that individuals gain value and honor through individual achievement. It is a lens through which we see our world.

THE TRUTH IN INDIVIDUALISM

1. Individualism acknowledges the extent of our freedom and the responsibility that comes with freedom. Our world confronts us with an ever-increasing number of limits to our freedom. Even an act as simple as crossing the street requires that you go to a designated place until signaled across by a bunch of synchronized lights. Otherwise you are likely to be hit by automobiles traveling within mandated lanes at legal speeds, driven by people obligated to possess a government-supplied license and lawfully bound to wear seatbelts. (If you don't, as both authors can attest, jaywalking fines can be steep.) Outside forces impose themselves on so many aspects of our lives that it is easy to convince ourselves that we no longer have any freedom.

While advocates of individualism generally seek to reduce external restrictions, they also remind us that we have internal freedoms that cannot be taken away. During World War II, Victor Frankl was one of the many millions of Jews subjected to the horrors of concentration camps. At one point he had been taken to a room, stripped of his clothes, seated on a chair in a darkened room with one light bulb shining on him. As his interrogators circled him and peppered him with questions, it dawned on him he had lost everything—his wife, children, home, money, freedom and now even his clothing. However, he still had the freedom to choose how he would respond. That was the one thing his captors could not take from him.

Is it possible that Frankl was freer than his captors? As odd as this question sounds, we know that many forms of captivity do not involve literal imprisonment. It is reasonable to believe that not everyone who worked in the Nazi concentration camps really wanted to treat other human beings as they did. They believed they had no choice. In other words, just as Frankl was compelled to do certain things against his will, many of his captors felt compelled by external forces to act as they did. However, who has greater freedom to determine how they will respond to those external compulsions?

In its best forms, individualism reminds us that responsibility is not limited to situations in which conditions are favorable. While it acknowledges that we are often subject to forces beyond our power, and that the people and institutions that should care for and protect us often fail in those duties, individualism accepts no excuses. If my unique goals give meaning to my life, I am ultimately responsible for the outcomes.

The linchpin for this high degree of responsibility is individualism's view of freedom, which focuses on our inner liberty to respond to even the worst circumstances. Thus, while many of Frankl's fellow prisoners gave up hope and died under trying conditions, Frankl relied on his inner freedom. He chose to dream about a hoped-for reunion with his wife and children. After his release, when he discovered that his wife and children had died in the concentration camps, he again drew on his internal freedom to overcome tragedy. He became famous for an innovative psychological approach called Logotherapy, which emphasizes our enormous autonomy to respond to whatever circumstances confront us.

Downplaying responsibility for our lives is always a significant temptation because so many things elude our direct control. However, most people share the intuition that even in the midst of strong forces at work in our lives, we still have freedom and responsibility. Individualism does us a favor by recognizing that freedom is not completely dependent on favorable circumstances. When we acknowledge this, the high degree of responsibility individualism assigns to each person follows naturally. Although we will argue later that individualism goes off track by defining the self as the primary target of our responsibility, the idea that we are obligated to care for our own physical, emotional, social, mental and spiritual well-being is admirable.

2. Individualism affirms my need to make a difference. One of our enduring cultural beliefs is that one person can make a difference. While individualism often presents a distorted picture of true heroism, it does recognize within each of us an impulse to do and be something significant. It is not an accident that every age has its stories about world-changers, exemplars and superheroes. The desire to leave our mark on the world seems to be built right into our DNA.

Working within the college context, we often encounter students who feel the tension between the desire to live on the edge and leave a unique legacy, or simply slip into a comfortable life of conformity. Individualism encourages us to dream big, take risks and aim at something beyond the status quo. When it moves us to question the way things are and creates dissatisfaction with mediocrity, individualism's emphasis on carving a new path and striving for excellence appeals to our deep desire to find our own type of heroism.

3. Individualism recognizes the strength of chosen beliefs. Will you have a stronger sense of commitment to beliefs that you have freely chosen or to beliefs that are forced on you? You probably think that this is a rhetorical question, and it is. It only makes sense that we gain a greater sense of ownership of a worldview, philosophy, religion or political commitment that we have embraced through our own decision.

Yet we do not have to go very far back in history to find the principle of *cuius regio eius religio* ("Whose kingdom, his religion") in full force. Under this principle, subjects within a given region must adopt their ruler's religion or face persecution. Even in recent years, we have seen how the various religious groups around the world have forced their views on those without power.

Because of their keen awareness of the dangers of state-sponsored religions and hereditary monarchies that were frequently abusive of citizens, the early immigrants who settled in what became the United States created a novel system. The new nation separated the institutional powers of government from religion and made citizens responsible for legislation of social rules. This created a fertile seedbed for individualism because each person was free to choose one's own political, social and religious views and affiliations. A common justification for this new political system was that people will have a higher degree of loyalty to ideas that are chosen rather than mandated.

Today, many Christians in the United States are disturbed by the religious pluralism in this country. However, for those who find this problematic, it is useful to remember that religious pluralism is built into our political system to keep government out of religious matters and allow individuals to choose their affiliations without coercion. To adopt a different system creates tremendous problems, not the least of which is a half-hearted commitment to beliefs imposed by outside powers. Moreover, it might be useful to remember that Christianity had its beginnings in a religiously pluralistic world (and one in which persecution was often a reality), and it did quite well within that environment. To a large measure, this was precisely due to the fact that the early Christians had to make a difficult, conscious decision to embrace this faith. To broaden the scope, individualism makes a strong case that freely chosen beliefs, whether political, religious or moral, are generally held with greater conviction.

THE POTENTIAL PROBLEMS OF INDIVIDUALISM

1. Individualism is constructed on a flawed view of reality. Three benchmark convictions of individualism are that the self is the universe's ultimate reality, each individual should seek self-sufficiency, and we control our own destiny. These are what philosophers call metaphysical claims. Metaphysics is simply a big word that refers to reality, and since reality is a pretty big deal perhaps it deserves a big word. While we don't intend to go into an in-depth discussion of metaphysics, we do believe that individualism's metaphysics requires a reality check.

Let's begin our reality check by taking a quick mental inventory of our surroundings. As an individual human being, I am only one of more than six billion human inhabitants on a very insignificant planet in an extremely small corner of an almost inconceivably massive cosmos. In relation to the age of this universe, my lifespan is, at best, a mere blink. I face any number of threats—accidents, disease, war and terrorism—that could shorten even farther the comparatively meager number of years I have on this planet. So how well does individualism's ideal of the in-control, self-sufficient, individual-human-being-as-primary-reality fit with this picture?

In an old *Calvin & Hobbes* comic strip, Calvin is gazing into an immense starry night sky and shouts, "I AM SIGNIFICANT," and immediately mutters softly, "Said the dust speck." Coming from a kid like Calvin, it's funny. However, for any adult with even a vague awareness of how vast the universe (not to mention the universe's Creator) is in comparison to our individual existence, the idea of mere dust specks shouting about their significance is just kind of pitiful.

Our quick mental tour of the realities of the universe should also swiftly put to rest the idea that we are in control and independent of external forces. We do not generate the air we breathe, create the soil that grows our food, or adjust the planet's distance from the sun or the tilt on its axis that guarantees a livable climate. And this only scratches the surface of our basic survival requirements. To recite the litany of the ways, both big and small, that our lives are reliant on things and people beyond ourselves would be mind-boggling.

The myth that we can and should be in control and self-sufficient is attractive. When we admit that we are subject to and dependent on so many external forces, we tap into our deepest fears. If I am not in control, who or what is in charge? Can those forces be trusted to have my interests in mind? What does the future hold for me? In times of relative security and stability, we can maintain illusions of control and self-sufficiency, although even then they are illusion. However, events like the terrorist attacks of September 11, 2001, confront us with the reality that our power to guide our lives is more limited than we would like to think.

2. Individualism is constructed on a flawed view of human nature. To be fair individualism occasionally recognizes that many events and situations cannot be completely steered by our own efforts. Thus, more sophisticated forms of individualism focus on the internal aspects of control. One of the most enduring anthems to this internal quest for self-sufficiency is William E. Henley's (1849-1903) poem "Invictus," part of which reads:

> Under the bludgeonings of chance,
> My head is bloody, but unbowed. . . .
> I am the master of my fate;
> I am the captain of my soul.

A similar lyrical expression of self-sufficiency was penned several years ago by Paul Simon. He uses metaphors such as wall, fortress, rock and island to speak of steeling ourselves against the pain that accompanies life's struggles and vicissitudes. However, Simon's "I Am a Rock" goes one step further than "Invictus" and speaks of the cost of self-sufficiency: "I have no need of friendship; / friendship causes pain. / It's laughter and it's loving I disdain."

Fortresses and walls are handy things for people who want to be "captains" of their own souls. However, fortresses are designed to keep people out, and this reveals the dark side of individual sovereignty. To remain in control and avoid the pain and disappointments that come when others fail us, "captains" and "masters" have to keep everyone else on the other side of the walls. We can do this, but Simon's words remind us that we will remain alone in our fortresses or on our islands.

Life and country music reveal two indisputable truths. First, something deep within us yearns for love. Second, we know that the relationships that bring the promise of love also hold the potential for great pain. In view of this, it is natural to want to control the terms of relationships in hopes of avoiding the damage that others can inflict on us. However, we immediately recognize the destruction that occurs when others attempt to control us. The bottom line is that without risk and freedom within relationships, genuine love is impossible. Since individualism fears the lack of control required by love, it presents a huge obstacle to our essential need for real love and relationships. The emptiness that results from individualism's fortress mentality tells us that the need for love embedded in human nature cannot be satisfied by this worldview.

3. Individualism has a flawed view of freedom and achievement. Individualism measures a person's value by performance. You set your own standards or goals and then appraise your worth against them. At least, that is the theory. But there is good reason to believe that we are not as independent in this process as the theory would imply.

The problem is most obvious for utilitarian individualists. First, their performance is judged by the standards and goals other people establish. Imagine a society in which athletic ability, earning power and intellectual achievement are not recognized as admirable or good. In fact, they are considered despicable and socially destructive. It seems clear that a utilitarian individualist in such a hypothetical world would not aspire to such athleticism, money or learning. Why? Because other people ultimately set the measure that determines what constitutes success. No utilitarian individualist succeeds without producing something that others see as valuable.

The expressive individualist is no less susceptible to this criticism. Whether one's sense of self-worth is found in working within the systems of social rules and values (utilitarian individualism) or in rebelling *against* them (expressive individualism), one is still ultimately dependent on standards determined by others. Thus, despite individualists' bluster about freedom and self-reliance, their self-worth is chained to the evaluations of other people.

The reality is that we are inherently social beings and even the individualist's self-image is determined by the perceptions and values of others. If the significance of my life is gauged by my accomplishments, whether judged as success within the social systems or through rebellion against them, the inescapable conclusion is that others ultimately determine whether I have succeeded. The only way out of this cycle is to look to a standard that transcends human life as a means of judging our life's value.

CONCLUSION

When a worldview is as deeply rooted in American culture as individualism is, it should not be surprising that it finds its way into the minds of Christians. This came home to me in a powerful way a number of years ago at a retreat. The speaker, a New Testament scholar, gave a devotional out of the Epistle to the Hebrews. At one point he observed that, after twenty-five years of studying Hebrews, it finally dawned on him that all the commands in this book, with one exception, are addressed to a community, not to individuals. I asked him, "Why did it take twenty-five years to discover this?" After all, unlike in the English language, the second person plural in Greek, used throughout Hebrews, is a different word than the second person singular. Immediately he identified the cause as individualism. Despite clear indicators in the text, the individualistic attitudes he absorbed from our culture led to the assumption that the commands directed at the church referred instead to individuals.

This example shows how influential a worldview can be once it is ingrained in culture, and this power is magnified by the fact that we are not conscious of its pull on our lives. As a result, it is difficult for us to feel like we are valuable unless we can point to an impressive list of accomplishments. We sing "Jesus loves me" so loud that it drowns out the proclamation that "God so loved the world." The word *freedom* generates thoughts of what we want to be free *from* rather than what we are free *for*. The Christian faith is reduced to *my* faith. Commitments to others are considered potential obstacles to happiness rather than a source of happiness. God becomes a power source for the achievement of my goals, but I never get around to asking how my life lines up with God's goals.

Because a worldview's power over us is magnified when we are not conscious of its influence, we need to keep important worldview questions in sight to keep from getting sidetracked. One of the first questions we need to ask about any worldview is, Who gets to be God? Individualism, by placing the individual at the center of the universe, attempts to put us in the God-position. Even if we will not say this explicitly, there is something attractive about imagining that we pull the strings in a universe that revolves around us. The comical and thought-provoking movie *Bruce Almighty* illustrates this desire. Bruce is deceptive, manipulative and punitive in his failed attempts to get the anchor position at the news station where he works. Finally, in receiving and using God's power, he brings about major events that land him this coveted position. He discovers it is not all that he thought it would be and comes to terms with his self-centered and controlling lifestyle. Standing before God, he is given another chance to forfeit his obsession for controlling things and to embrace a life of giving to others.

The Bible often speaks in paradoxes that sound like downright contradictions if heard through the filters of different worldviews. Thus, if one reads "For whoever wants to save his life will lose it, but whoever loses his life for me will find it" (Matthew 16:25) through the lens of individualism, it sounds absurd. If an individualist loses his life, the center of the universe collapses and all is lost. But Christianity says that we derive our value from a God who is the true center of the cosmos. Thus, when we lose our lives in this God, we are united with the God who stands in the heart of reality. This part of the Christian story stands in stark contrast to individualism's claims about our place in the order of things.

One other important element gets misplaced in an individualistic worldview. When I claim to be the primary reality in the universe, this requires that I see others either as a tool for maintaining my status or as a competitor for my place at the center. Others have only utilitarian value (they are valuable to the extent that they help me) or they are obstacles to my personal projects and goals. However, in the Christian story, God invites all to join and enjoy his kingdom. This is the secret to our social nature. God creates us to be in community, not just with him, but with all that he values. That changes everything. Others are no longer mere tools or hostile competitors, but fellow human beings assigned great value by the universe's true Center. As a result, one nonnegotiable in becoming a part of God's kingdom is recognizing that God's purposes are not primarily about *me*, but about *us*. This understanding of community puts Christianity on a collision path with individualism.

3

CONSUMERISM

I Am What I Own

THE BIBLE CLEARLY TEACHES AN IDEA you will seldom hear from the pulpit or in a Bible study. This idea, which Scripture lays out right from the beginning, is that God has created us as consumers. Moreover, God wants us to enjoy the process of consumption. Really! In Genesis 2, God created a human and then proceeded to give him the things he needed for a good life. "And the LORD God made all kinds of trees grow out of the ground—trees that were pleasing to the eye and good for food" (Genesis 2:9). Part of God's gift to Adam was a garden, and a beautiful one at that. God intended for Adam and Eve (who joined him a few verses later) to enjoy the garden's aesthetics and gain satisfaction when they ate (consumed) the products that grew in it.

Although we will fill out the picture of what human beings need later, this should not overshadow the fact that we cannot live without consuming certain things. At the most basic level, we have to consume things. It is an unavoidable fact that whatever we eat, drink, wear or live in must come from nature. This is not just the case for us, but for anything that has biological life. However, human beings are more than just biological beings, and fulfillment of our social, educational, cultural and spiritual needs and desires also requires that natural resources, to some degree, be rearranged or used. In short, life cannot be sustained or complete without consuming things. Therefore, assuming that life (and a complete one at that) is a good thing, it is impossible to say that the consumption that makes life possible is bad.

While Scripture and everyday experience make it clear that we must consume things as a means of preserving and enhancing our lives, there is always the danger that responsible consumption will degenerate into *consumerism*. This lived worldview is also sometimes referred to as *materialism*, although we will not use that term here to avoid confusion with scientific materialism (see chapter six), which is a very different thing. Consumerism is a worldview that starts with something that is a relative good—consumption—and makes it an absolute good. Consumerism absolutizes consumption by believing that we can find fulfillment by accumulating wealth and everything that comes with it. It tells us that all our needs can be satisfied by what we consume. The more we use, the more needs we satisfy. Since the fulfillment of needs is what salvation is about, consumerism is, in reality, a secular religion.

One unique feature of a consumerist worldview is that almost no one will admit that they believe that salvation can be found by acquiring and using things. However, the evidence of consumerism's impact on American life is overwhelming. The documentary *Affluenza* reveals that Americans have consumed more resources over the last fifty years than the total used by the entire population of earth prior to 1950. An average American consumes thirty times more that the average person from India. In 1999, teenagers spent a hundred billion dollars, and their parents spent an additional fifty billion dollars on them, according to the documentary film *Merchants of Cool*. We could cite a long list of similar statistics, but they would only confirm what is already obvious—we use much more than we actually need, and we know it. What we are often unclear about, however, is why we do this.

KEY CONVICTIONAL BELIEFS OF CONSUMERISM

Accumulating and using things brings fulfillment. Each of us desires a fulfilling, satisfying and meaningful life. People may differ in their opinions about what is fulfilling or satisfying, but we all find a certain degree of satisfaction in many things we own and consume. Moreover, we attach meaning to the objects we own. A car is not just a car; it may mean freedom, status or security for us. Attaching meaning to things is, in itself, not a bad thing. In fact, it is unavoidable. Where we cross the line into consumerism is when we adopt the idea that *all* our relevant needs are fulfilled by the meaning we attach to the accumulation and use of things.

Several years ago, Ford Motor Company produced a fascinating advertisement that played on our desire for fulfillment. In the background was a Ford Ranger Super Cab with all four doors open. A surf board, a kayak, snow skis, a mountain bike, a sleeping bag, climbing implements, an electric guitar and amplifier, scuba equipment and fishing gear were displayed in front of the truck. A young man sat in the middle of all of this paraphernalia, legs crossed and arms and hands in an open position like he was meditating. The advertisement read as follows:

> Spence put a new twist on an old philosophy. To be one with everything, he says, you've got to have one of everything. That's why he also has the new Ford Ranger. So he can seek wisdom on a mountain top. Take off in hot pursuit of enlightenment. And connect with Mother Earth. By looking no further than into the planet's coolest 4-door compact pickup. He says it gives him access to inner peace. Which makes him one happy soul.

From a marketing perspective, this is a great ad. It taps into a market of young men who enjoy being active, while also giving a nod in the general direction of our need for spiritual fulfillment. The implication, however, is that inner peace and happiness is dependent on having one of everything, especially the new Ford Ranger. Blurring the lines between the material and spiritual is a very successful sales tactic. It is also a part of the larger conviction in our culture (although usually unspoken) that you can buy fulfillment, or at least that fulfillment cannot be attained without the proper commodities.

This conviction is also revealed in advertising that implies that only the "right gift" (i.e., a really expensive gift) will communicate how special your spouse, children or parents are. A diamond ring or necklace is portrayed as evidence of how much a man loves his wife. A new Mercedes as a Christmas present communicates one's deepest affections. The primary message is that the way to show someone how deeply you love and appreciate them is to give them expensive things. Reading between the lines, the more expensive the thing, the more you love that person. Once again, the border separating consumer goods from love gets fuzzy.

Money is power. Money provides access to different types of power, and consumerism is built on the assumption that the forms of power attainable by wealth are desirable. At its most basic level, money provides the purchasing power to get the food, clothing and shelter we need. The more money you have, the more options it creates for you in terms of where you live, what you eat and the clothes you wear. Beyond the basics, my financial worth determines the make and model of car I drive, the college I attend, the freedom to travel when and where I would like, and a myriad of other things.

Money also creates power in the form of status. Let's be honest. We want others to view us as significant, and money plays a key role in how others see us. A contemporary symbol of status is the Hummer. Most of the Hummers you see never make it off the freeway even though their ability to get us into the most inaccessible places is featured prominently in all the ads. So why do we buy them? Could it be that they are seen as an expression of our financial clout? Consumerism keeps score of how we value different professions, and the people in them, by the size of the paycheck attached to these professions and what that paycheck allows its owner to acquire.

Money also provides the power to protect ourselves against some of the uncertainties of life. Perhaps one of the best examples is our preoccupation with insurance. Any tangible goods you possess can be insured, whether it is your life, your home, your car or your pedigreed Schnauzer's teeth. Some of this is a matter of prudence and responsibility, but if you take quick stock of how much money goes toward the pursuit of security, you will also discover how fearful and insecure we are about losing our things. Fear of losing our stuff, in turn, reveals how much value we have attached to it. Consumerism seeks to convince us that the answer to insecurity is a matter of purchasing the right types of protection against potential threats. If our identities are wrapped up in what we own, losing our possessions means we lose something of ourselves.

Money also possesses another unique form of influence—the power to define what we should consider important. And indicators point toward a trend in which wealth increasingly defines itself as the most important goal to pursue. Since 1969 Dr. Alexander Astin has surveyed college freshmen. In the early 1970s, about 70 percent of young people went to college to develop a meaningful philosophy of life. Today, this has dropped to 40 percent. However, 75 percent of current freshmen say they go to college to be very well off financially.[1] What has happened here is not that the desire to bolster our net worth has become more important than developing a meaningful philosophy of life. Instead, the aim of being well off financially (the roots of consumerism) has *become* a philosophy of life for many. In the process, consumerism has reshaped the way we understand the role of education, just as it does almost every other structure of life. Money defines our world, if we let it.

Just a little bit more. Anyone who resides in the Western world has to acknowledge that the majority of us have more than sufficient resources to take care of our basic survival needs. At the same time, we still strive to acquire more. What is behind this? If we view money as the source of freedom, status and security, it is a short step from here to the idea that the more we have, the better off we will be. John D. Rockefeller, one of the wealthiest people in the world at the time, summed up this attitude when he was asked how much money is enough. His reply: "just a little bit more."

When consumerism asserts that "just a little bit more" is what we should seek, it is wise to ask, just a little bit more *of what?* Since consumerism defines our needs in terms of money and what it can obtain, the pursuit of more of what can be purchased and quantified becomes its core value. Thus, corporations define *more* as profit, churches think of *more* in terms of buildings and warm bodies in the pews, and con-

---

[1]"A Long Way from Flower Power," *Economist*, January 17, 1998, p. 26. Quoted in Tom Sine, *Mustard Seed Versus McWorld* (Grand Rapids: Baker, 1999), p. 95.

sumers understand *more* as consumer goods. The good life becomes a matter of totaling up the numbers.

When Martha Stewart's company went public in 1999 it nearly doubled in price in one day, making her net worth hundreds of millions of dollars. "Just a little bit more" is perhaps what Martha Stewart and stockbroker Peter Bacanovic were thinking when they made a stock trade based on an insider's tip and then lied to cover up what they had done. The irony is that the "well-timed trade" saved her around fifty thousand dollars, a relatively small amount compared to the massive damage to her overall financial worth from the resulting drop in her own company's value. Add five months in jail, five months under house arrest and two years' probation, and she paid a very high price for her desire to acquire just a little bit more.

Wealthy institutions and individuals are the easy targets when it comes to criticism for the pursuit of wealth at the cost of all other values. However, we don't have to have a large net worth to adopt a consumerist worldview. While the poorest have valid needs for basic goods, when they believe that money is *the* solution to their search for fulfillment, they have bought into consumerism as deeply as anyone else. This brings us back around to the enduring desire for more in this worldview. As our acquisitions increase, so does our definition of *need*. Both rich and poor can play the consumerism game because no matter how much we accumulate, whether power, status, security or financial assets, we always want more.

People are viewed as objects to consume. While most people would not voice this conviction, the natural outgrowth of full-blown consumerism is that people are reduced to objects and can be used in ways that bring about our own gratification. A blatant example of this appeared in the last quarter of 2003, when Carl's Jr. developed a series of advertisements that featured Hugh Hefner and several beautiful women, including his wife. The basic message was that, just as Hugh Hefner likes variety in women, he also likes variety in his hamburgers. There it was: people end up in the same category as burgers. Hefner, probably more than any other person over the last fifty years, has made a business out of turning women into objects of gratification, so it was jolting to see him as a spokesperson for hamburgers. Even more jolting, however, is that our culture has moved so far toward accepting the objectification of human beings that a major company feels safe running commercials that so openly compare women and consumables such as burgers.

The tendency to treat people as objects or as means toward some other end is also evident in other ways. Parents fight the temptation to confuse a child's inherent worth with his or her performance in school or sports. As we lose the internal guides that remind us of the value of human life, we have had to erect more external barriers and rules to make sure that people are not treated like lab rats, and we seem to be chipping away at these rules. We are affirmed when we produce more at work, but rarely are we affirmed when we turn down overtime because of family commitments. Christian organizations are no exception to the temptation to objectify people. The demands for work performance often crowd out an employee's pursuit of the very spiritual values these groups claim as their core principles. In sum, the influence of consumerism makes it difficult to value people because they are made in the image of God. If the fulfillment of my needs and desires determines my goals, others have value only to the extent that they allow us to reach those goals.

I discard what ceases to fulfill me or meet my needs. If consumerism dictates that we value things and people only when they are useful for achieving personal fulfillment, it follows that whatever is not useful in that pursuit can and should be discarded. We've become quite accomplished at this. The documentary *Affluenza* states that Americans throw away enough each year to fill a convoy of garbage trucks half way to the moon, including seven million cars and enough aluminum cans to make six thousand DC-10 airplanes. Every year!

It is hard to deny that we have become quite comfortable with disposing of whatever we believe we no longer need. When we combine this with consumerism's tendency to reduce people to the level of objects, we would also expect to find a corresponding tendency to view people as disposable. Even though it is an extreme example, the popular show *Survivor* tapped into this very idea. The premise of the show is to use other people to help you survive until the next episode. When any individual becomes a liability, the others turn on that person and vote him or her off the team.

While real life is usually not as blatant as *Survivor*, relationships seem to be increasingly thought of in transactional terms. Instead of thinking about friendship or marriage as relationships with intrinsic value, we look to them as a means of fulfilling our needs. When the needs are no longer satisfied by that relationship, we discard it and move on to another that we believe will be a better use of our resources. Instead of placing value on commitment, we constantly search for what is novel and interesting.

THE GOOD IN CONSUMERISM

One thing that consumerism gets right is obvious. Human beings have needs that are directly addressed by consumption. A useful tool for understanding the relationship between consumption and needs has been provided by Abraham Maslow. His hierarchy of human needs begins with the basic physiological and safety needs, proceeding to needs for belonging and love. Above this, we have a need for self-esteem and status. At the top of this pyramid is the need for what he calls self-actualization (if you like, you could substitute the word *salvation* here). The lowest needs in Maslow's hierarchy tend to occupy our attention until they are met. Only then can we move up the scale to focus on higher needs. We might argue about whether this is the way things *should* be, but it is not hard to accept this as a generally accurate picture of what actually happens. If we are hungry, extremely tired or under physical threat, we are not the most loving and sociable creatures.

If Maslow's hierarchy of human needs reflects reality, even imperfectly, it helps us understand the positive side of consumption as well as the lure of consumerism as a worldview. You will notice that at the bottom of the pyramid, the most basic needs are tied to consumption. Food and clothing are physical necessities; we use what we find in nature to fill those needs. In other words, there is an almost one-to-one correspondence between using material goods and satisfying a need at this fundamental level. As we move up the scale to our need for friendship or respect from others, for example, the link with physical goods is still there, although less basic. The point is that consumerism is correct when it notes that all human beings have essential needs that are connected with consumption. The temptation, which we will examine later, is to interpret every need as one that can be quenched by accumulation and consumption.

1. I determine how to use my resources. Part of being an adult is a greater level of freedom to make decisions than we had as a child. This freedom creates demands for important decisions. How will we earn our money? What will we do with it once we get it? What should we expect from it? In turn, our decisions about wealth and our use of it involve many other judgments, such as the type of education we will pursue, how we will use our time and energy and where we will live. In other words, consumerism helps us remember that wealth is closely linked with certain types of freedom.

Of course, freedom itself is not a pure good, even if we sometimes speak of it as such. In fact, if you give some people more freedom, bad things can happen, which is why we limit the freedom of children and criminals. Increased freedom only works toward good if combined with responsibility. The bottom line is that consumerism, by making us aware of the broad array of uses for our resources, confronts us with choices and reminds us that we have significant freedom in how we make those choices. This seems to be an important part of the creation story, where God pays a huge compliment to human beings by giving them freedom to make choices about how they use the resources God has created. God also compliments us by making human beings responsible for their decisions. In short, the vast number of options presented in a consumerist society can serve as a reminder of how much freedom we have and the level of responsibility that comes with it (even if consumerism's worldview doesn't provide useful guidance about how we make responsible decisions).

2. Consumerism promotes competition and new ideas. A positive aspect of living in a society with such vast resources, and the options made available through them, is that the competition for our dollars can be beneficial. Those who make things that can be sold want to keep selling their products, and more of them. In order to do that, market forces compel producers to make things that people will want to buy. This can result in a great deal of innovation. This isn't difficult to illustrate. For those of us who started buying computers a long time ago (in computer years), it is a marvel how powerful and cheap they have become. Many of the basic services and goods we need are more readily available, in better quality and at lower prices than before. And who knows how many years we will add to our lifespan by innovations in medical technology? While we should not forget that consumerism's benefits often come at significant costs in other areas, it is hard to deny that demand for newer, better and cheaper goods drives creativity and new ideas, and we often derive great benefit from these innovations.

Problems with Consumerism

1. Consumerism is reductionistic in defining our needs. Abraham Maslow, whom we met above, is credited with saying that if all you own is a hammer, everything starts to look like a nail. A hammer is a great tool for driving nails (including thumbnails, I've discovered), but it can be a horribly destructive thing if used for jobs not designed for hammers. The same is true for money. It can do a great deal of good if used in proper ways, but when consumerism defines every problem as one that can be solved by wealth and its byproducts, you get very bad results. Another way of stating this is to say that consumerism is reductionistic. It reduces everything—our needs, our understanding of people and relationships, even God—to categories that can be addressed or resolved by the use of wealth. This reduction distorts the true value of everything. The ironic result, then, is that in its quest for power and security, consumerism actually produces impotence and fear. We will briefly examine this process.

The first form of reductionism we mention above is consumerism's tendency to reduce our needs to a single category. A fundamental problem with this limited definition of needs can be illustrated by returning to Maslow's hierarchy of human needs. Maslow points out what we already know from experience: Human beings have important needs that correspond with every level of our existence—social, psychological, moral, intellectual, economic, physiological and spiritual. Consumerism tempts us to believe that all these aspirations can be filled by products we can charge to a credit card.

While we have acknowledged that some of our needs can be sufficiently addressed by financial means, consumerism encounters serious problems when needs arise that cannot be resolved by money. This forces consumerism to make substitutions. Since virtue cannot be purchased, consumerism tells us that a lot of money will make us socially respectable. Money won't buy love, but it can pay for sex. Immortality is not for sale, but health care, life insurance and large headstones are. You can't pay enough to buy God, but a solid church budget can guarantee that you can get a preacher who can talk about God in an engaging way.

Of course, the problem with buying substitutes is that they do not address our real needs. When we try to get love, friendship, genuine respect and spiritual vitality from consumer goods, we find that they cannot deliver. The real need is still there. This is why consumerism is so closely linked with a relentless demand for a little bit more. Consumerism tells us that the holes in our lives will be filled if we just have more. Getting just a bit more proves to be unsatisfying, however, because money never fills legitimate needs for intellectual growth, moral virtue, love, true esteem and God. A counterfeit never replaces the real thing.

A second form of consumeristic reductionism is its depersonalization of what should be kept personal. When I was a pastor, a young couple came for help with relationship struggles. At one point I asked them to tell me about their priorities. The young woman said that, without question, her fiancé was most important to her. She would do anything for him and was, in fact, spending a lot time working on a house he had bought as an investment. Her fiancé, in contrast, said that becoming financially secure was the most important priority in his life. As he looked at her and said, "Financial security is even more important to me than my relationship with you," an unforgettable look of deep betrayal came to her face. This young woman realized there could be no meaningful relationship when she, as a person, ranked lower on his scale of priorities than financial security. She wisely broke off the engagement.

The depersonalizing power of money also takes on a corporate dimension when imbalances in wealth distribution create an imbalance in the way we value people. Thus, as Jacques Ellul points out, "Poverty . . . leads to the total alienation of the poor, an alienation which puts the labor force at the disposal of the wealthy, permitting the wealthy to impose their own law and conception of life, their own thought and religion."[2] Of course, we are willing to bet that few wealthy people (in global terms, that includes anyone with sufficient income to buy this book or sufficient time to write such a book) have any intention of oppressing others. If we are honest, though, it is hard to avoid the conclusion that inequalities in wealth create situations where people are reduced to commodities.

Even with the best of intentions, it is difficult to avoid treating people as commodities, because we like what others can do for us. To put it in more raw language, it is tempting to use people for our goals. Thus, we may view work colleagues in terms of our own advancement or think of our marriages from the perspective of personal satisfaction. This would all be perfectly proper if people were objects, because objects are intended to be used for our benefit. However, because human beings are persons, not objects, our relationships must also take account of others' needs. Personal relationships involve both give and take. Because consumerism views other people as a means by which we can get what we want, it turns them into objects.

The third type of reductionism involves displacing God with money. Jesus recognizes the temptation toward this reduction when he says, "You cannot serve both God and Money" (Matthew 6:24). If we allow it, mammon (money) becomes a rival god because it claims to do the same things we are called to rely on God for. Mammon promises security, status and power. In return, it asks for our allegiance. Mammon is never happy with a subordinate role. Instead, it contends for our deepest commitment.[3] Because our deepest commitments should be reserved for God alone, when our consumeristic pursuits take first place in our lives, they become a secular form of religion. But mammon is a de-

---

[2]Jacques Ellul, *Money and Power* (Downers Grove, Ill.: InterVarsity Press, 1984), p. 78.
[3]Richard J. Foster, *Money, Sex, and Power* (San Francisco: Harper and Row, 1985), p. 28.

manding god. Regardless of the net worth on the balance sheet, his salvation always requires "a little bit more."

2. Consumerism redefines our values. The story is told of Dominic, a monk who founded the Dominican order, and his visit to Pope Innocent III in Rome in the thirteenth century. While giving Dominic a tour of the Vatican, in which its massive treasures were prominently displayed, the Pope said (in reference to Acts 3:6), "Peter [signifying the Pope] can no longer say, 'Silver and gold have I none.'" Dominic responded, "Neither can he say, 'Rise and walk.'" Dominic's point is that when we value the types of power available through wealth, we also devalue power of a different, and more important, sort.

If it is the case (and it is) that those who once valued the spiritual power available from God can eventually exchange it for monetary power, we should understand the process by which this occurs. A good way to gauge what we value is to ask ourselves what we are most afraid of losing. This can be a revealing exercise, because anyone who carefully reflects on life recognizes our impotence against a wide variety of threats. You name the area, we feel vulnerable and out of control—security against crime and natural disaster, making the next mortgage or school payment, health concerns, the influences on our children, our reputation with peers. The list can go on forever. If you want to know just how fearful we are, listen carefully to the advertisers. They are keenly aware of our insecurities about everything from unpleasant bodily odors to our very lives.

In the face of all these uncertainties, we naturally seek to avoid and eliminate threatening situations. This is where things get tricky, because it is our responsibility to assert control over certain aspects of our lives and the environments around us, and money used within proper limits can be very useful. The danger comes when money creates the illusion that all things are potentially under our control. It fools us into thinking that if we just had sufficient financial resources (always "a little bit more" than we already have) we could be in the driver's seat and the threats would disappear.

Our desire to be in the driver's seat encounters two major problems, however. First, consumerism is unrealistic about the extent of our power. An honest appraisal will tell us quickly that most threats to our well-being cannot be stopped by acquiring stuff or throwing money at them. The most obvious case is death. Under consumerism, the bottom line is survival, because all our fears are wrapped around our continuing existence. But even the wealthiest individuals know that they will die, and while they might be able to postpone it for a while, there's ultimately nothing they (and we) can do about it. Second, consumerism's drive to control things forgets that we are not the ultimate source or owners of what we have. While the products we buy may have labels that say Nabisco, Dell or Lexus on them, God is ultimately the source of the materials from which these things come. Moreover, even though we may have legal property rights over the things we purchase, the Bible reminds us that God has ultimate ownership. This is one of the important lessons of the Garden of Eden. The humans who inhabited the garden had the privilege of enjoying it, but they were middle management. The garden was owned by God. Therefore their privilege was balanced by their responsibility to be good caretakers for the owner, who happens to care deeply for his creation. To put it otherwise, then, consumerism, which lays claim to what rightly comes from and belongs to God, is just one more form of misguided pride.

Misguided pride is dangerous enough precisely because it is pride, but it is doubly dangerous because it is misguided. If we take a look at the result of living according to the consumeristic worldview, the search for security, power and fame actually produce very different results. Those who amass more money end up buying increasingly more complex vaults and hiring more bodyguards. Those with power are anxious about what will happen if they lose power. The famous hire publicists to make sure that people will continue to adore them, and then hire bodyguards to protect them from the people who adore them. Since we never have enough of anything that money can generate, it is never a real solution to our insecurity, our sense of powerlessness and our fear of insignificance.

CONCLUSION

At the beginning of the chapter, we noted that God creates us in such a way that the use and enjoyment of consumables is grounded in our humanity. Moreover, if we take the incarnation seriously, where God assumes a real humanity in the person of Jesus, it follows naturally that Jesus also had physical needs such as air, food and shelter, and it should not be too much of a stretch to believe that Jesus enjoyed quite a number of here-and-now activities. In short, the incarnation confirms what is clear in creation. Consumption is endorsed by God, as long as it is kept in its proper place.

The creation story also helps us develop a proper perspective on consumption when it defines us as middle managers, or "stewards," of creation. As stewards, we stand between God, the Creator and owner of all, and the creation he loves. This location tells us that we have responsibilities that run in two directions. In our managerial duties, our task is to act for the benefit of creation, which includes the others who inhabit this planet with us. We thus violate our responsibilities when we abuse that which is placed under our care. Our role is to use the resources of nature, but to use them wisely and with a view to the concerns of the owner.

The owner of nature, God, has concerns about his creation. Because of our responsibility toward God, our stewardship of creation is not separate from our spirituality, but is integrated into our spiritual existence. Thus, pious-sounding talk about how "all we need is God" can lead to a false understanding of spirituality. God created us with various needs—biological, social, psychological, spiritual and economic—and provided for their fulfillment in a variety of ways. This is why Christian ministries that feed the hungry, provide shelter to the homeless, fight injustice and bring reconciliation are valid. This is the element of truth in consumerism that makes it attractive. It recognizes that every person has real physical needs, and God is quite concerned that those needs are met. Thus, while we are critical of consumerism because it looks at the human being only from the perspective of our material needs, we should also be critical of any form of Christianity that ignores these needs.

When we talk of our role as stewards, words like *duty* and *responsibility* arise often, and we think this is fundamental to understanding our place in creation. Managers are expected to make good decisions and are provided with a certain amount of freedom to do just that. God treats us in the same way. While God gives us certain broad guidelines about how to handle our financial resources, we are not provided with a magic formula that tells us exactly what to do in every case. We are expected to use our honest and thoughtful discretion.

So how do we balance our responsibility to care for our financial and consumption needs without falling into consumerism? Where do we cross the line between proper management of God's resources and abusive pride? That is a hard question to answer. Let us illustrate with a couple of rather mundane examples from our own lives. Mark enjoys cycling and owns a bike worth about twelve hundred dollars. It has provided a way for him to keep in shape, brings him a lot of personal enjoyment, and he intended to ride it on an extended trip to raise money to purchase a van for Foothill AIDS Project, an organization that works with individuals who are HIV positive and their families. (Unfortunately, an accident two weeks before the trip prevented him from riding, but he accompanied the others who made the ride.) Steve likes good coffee, and often passes up the free stuff in the office for the better-tasting brew he can buy elsewhere. Over time, the venti decafs can add up to enough cash for a twelve-hundred-dollar bike.

In both cases, we have some rather expensive pleasures, and we have to decide whether our consumption is justifiable in a world where people starve to death for want of basic needs. Of course, when you put it this way, it sounds pretty hard to justify these expenses. And that is exactly the type of struggle involved for Christians. Are these purchases justified or just rationalized? It is hard to tell because Scripture does not give us a concrete set of "right answers" for making these and all the other consumption decisions that confront us daily.

Perhaps the best we can do is to continue the struggle with several things in mind, a number of which have already been mentioned. We must remember that our decisions about consumption are made in the presence of God, which makes financial choices a matter of our spirituality. Consumption is part of God's design for us, but it is only part of God's design. One of the most difficult factors in our decision-making is being candid with ourselves about why we make the financial decisions we make, so a good process requires a lot of honest self-examination. We place ourselves in grave danger if we don't recognize the influences that constantly pull us toward consumerism. Moreover, a Christian view of money requires a global perspective about our consumption and awareness that our choices have far-reaching ripple effects, effects that we may not even see.

Finally, in light of the last point, it is worth noting that we don't talk much at all about our financial affairs with others. In view of everything Scripture says about the dangers of consumerism, its link between our stewardship and our spirituality, and our need for accountability to a community, it seems to follow that we should be more open with other believers about our struggles to understand how to be good managers of what God entrusts us with.

It is probably not an overstatement to say that consumerism is the most potent competitor to a Christian worldview in our culture. The forces that push us in that direction are pervasive, and our wealth has gradually made us more accustomed to reliance on our financial resources. It is also dangerous because consumerism exists mostly underground. Few will admit to embracing it as a plan of salvation. However, every now and then, it pokes its head up into clear view. For example, a few years ago, it was not uncommon to see bumper stickers that proclaimed, "The one who dies with the most toys wins." The major problem with this worldview, whether you confess it openly or simply live as if it is true, is that no matter how many toys you accumulate, in the end, you have only toys. Toys are great as long as we understand their limitations and use them accordingly. When they take the place of God, however, they fail to bring satisfaction.

4

NATIONALISM

My Nation, Under God

IF JESUS WERE ALIVE TODAY, would he be patriotic? Got your answer? Actually, that is not really the question I want to pursue. What interests me is whether you assumed that I was asking whether Jesus would be a patriotic *American?* Of course, we are aware that Jesus was not an American during his earthly life, so there is no reason to think that he would be an American if he was alive today. In fact, odds are slim that he would be a U.S. citizen. This country is home to only about 3 to 4 percent of the world's population, and there are almost two hundred recognized nations. Furthermore, we know that when Jesus did reside on this planet, his place of birth was not one of that era's superpowers.

I readily admit that my follow-up question about Jesus' patriotism toward the United States is not entirely fair. Since most who read this book will be U.S. citizens, it is natural to ponder the question within our own frame of reference. At the same time, it is important to consider also whether it is uncomfortable to think that Jesus might have been born into another nation had his incarnation occurred today, because the idea that one's own nation is uniquely favored by God and an integral part of God's plan (an idea known as exceptionalism) holds the seeds of a religious nationalism.

Religious nationalism is rather distinctive among the worldviews surveyed in this book because, in this country, it is most frequently found within conservative Christian circles. Our superpower status and the longevity of our political system provide a potent seedbed for nationalist ideas. When this is combined with a rather widespread belief that the United States is (or in some cases, was) a Christian nation, nationalism becomes a seductive worldview for Christians. To be sure, not all forms of nationalism are religious in orientation, but for reasons we will examine below, most are.

When we speak of nationalism as a lived worldview in competition with Christianity, this should not be taken as a condemnation of patriotism. We want to say as explicitly and forcefully as we can that patriotism, the love of one's country, is a good and necessary thing. However, we want to say just as forcefully that a patriotism that loses perspective and offers our highest loyalty to a specific state is an evil and destructive thing. In essence, nationalism is the imbalanced and distorted form of something that is good—patriotism. There is no simple way to determine with precision when good patriotism degenerates into nationalism, but we will attempt to give some potential benchmarks for self-examination. Before we get to that, however, it is important to take a closer look at the nature of nations so we can understand why religion, perhaps our own, is so often co-opted by nationalism.

NATION CREATION

Nations are not eternal entities. They come into and go out of existence. Thus, a vital theme in our discussion is that nations are created things, and rather artificial creations at that. For example, what has been included within the borders of the United States and under the jurisdiction of its laws has varied significantly within its relatively brief history. Through rebellion, settlement, purchase, conquest, annexation and transition from territory to state, the map of this country has gone through numerous forms. Even though we think of its borders as relatively stable now, history should remind us that it is unlikely that "the

United States of America" will refer to exactly the same land mass a century in the future, and it may not exist at all. If you find this hard to imagine, compare a globe from a hundred years ago with a current one. You will get the picture.

Nations are not simply artificial in the sense that borders are often fluid and the means by which they are established is frequently arbitrary. No single justification exists to explain why one group of people becomes associated with one particular nation rather than another. Sometimes nations are defined by old colonial structures or a common history. In other cases, linguistic, cultural, traditional, tribal, racial or religious commonalities provide the basis for nationhood. In Australia and other island countries, borders are established by geography, even though the people within those geographical boundaries differ radically on numerous levels. In yet other cases, the elements above are the very things that must be transcended in order for a nation to emerge. In America's early history, the diverse linguistic, cultural, religious and historical backgrounds of people in the colonies made unity extremely difficult. Initially, then, harmony was found in common goals or ideals, such as liberty and equality. Over time, however, much of the United States' national identity has shifted from these common ideals to include also a common history. In short, national character is not a static thing but something that changes over time. The point is twofold here: the raw materials for nation-creation vary widely from one country to another, and what provides the basis for the state in one circumstance may be the greatest obstacle to a cohesive state in another situation.

While the paragraph above speaks about just some of the ways nations find justification for becoming political entities with unique identities, it does not really tell us *why* nations come into being. At the risk of oversimplification, this question can be boiled down to power, which manifests itself in three closely related ways—stability, military power/defensibility and economic clout. Most of us do not think of the nation-state in the Western world as a modern phenomenon, but that is the reality. The feudalistic social structures that existed for much of the medieval period consisted of fluctuating confederations formed by minor nobility, each controlling small swaths of real estate. Similar types of systems are still found in parts of the world in which warlords or tribal groups hold actual control within the borders of a country. Now, as in the medieval period, these structures lack stability and all that goes with it. Nations promise, and have a greater capacity to deliver, the political, military and economic stability and strength that cannot be attained by smaller political units.

To say that power is the main reason for the existence of nations is not to pronounce judgment on it. The idea that political, military or economic power is an evil per se is far too simplistic. A lot of good results from political and social stability, military deterrence and economic strength; and patriotism is properly directed when it acknowledges these positive aspects. However, to achieve and maintain power, nations must secure the loyalty of citizens. Without this loyalty, the power and stability of the state is in jeopardy.

The means by which nations pursue power can lead to nationalism, so the tools used by a nation to legitimate itself become an important issue. Let's be honest. If a nation says, "We are a variable and artificial entity that sometimes fails in our moral duties, but we want your allegiance in order to increase our power and security," this is not a particularly effective way to gain the fervent loyalty of citizens. Instead, a nation seeks to win allegiance by attaching itself to something that gives it the credibility of the superior or the eternal. This can happen by making claims for a nation's ideals, people, history or something else. However, in most cases, appeal is made to the divine as the foundation for what is superior or eternal about a country. When God is viewed as the absolute authority, nations often attempt to co-opt this authority to give them legitimacy. This is why a nationalistic worldview is usually religious in nature and is generally adopted by individuals with a strong religious orientation. Out of its belief in some form of superiority, then, nationalists claim that God has given their country a special mission to the rest of the world.

A CASE STUDY IN NATIONALISM

Several elements mentioned above played a part in what is perhaps the most important historical development in the last century—the birth of the Nazi party in Germany. It is important to recall that the *N* in Nazi stood for "nationalist," and at the heart of German nationalism was belief in the superiority of the Aryan race. It portrayed the German *Volk* as the highest expression of humanity, and thus the destined rulers of all other races—on the basis of their preeminence in their history, intellectual accomplishments and moral nature. This was all linked to Christianity by proclaiming Jesus to be the true Aryan and the founder of a "positive Christianity" that had been lost when the Jewish Old Testament was attached to the Bible. Thus, the German nation was the conduit through which this purified Christianity would be reintroduced to the world. Through Germany, the world would receive the true religion.

These ideas were combined with a German tradition that encourages the obedience of the church to political authorities. This resulted in a system intended to unite all the Protestant churches in Germany under a single bishop, who was then accountable to "the leader" (i.e., the *Führer*), who was, of course, Hitler. The next step of this so-called German Christian movement was to expel all Christians of Jewish descent from ministry positions, and later from membership in church, so that a proper Aryan purity and positive Christianity could be attained. The extent to which significant parts of the German church was co-opted by nationalism can be seen in a resolution passed in 1933 by the Reich Church, which states in part: "God has created me a German. Germanism is a gift of God. God wants me to fight for my Germany. . . . The goal of the 'Faith Movement of "German Christians"' is an evangelical German Reich."

YOU MAY BE A NATIONALIST IF . . .

It is easy to look back on a nationalism as obviously destructive as Nazism and think we are immune from such nonsense. However, the history, traditions and the immense power of the United States hold potent factors that can and do lead to nationalistic tendencies. On balance, the story of the United States is, in our opinion, a good one, but that goodness is part of the danger. Nationalism becomes temptation precisely when nations have sufficient strength or goodness to inspire deep-seated loyalties. As a result, citizens of nations that arouse strong patriotism do not appreciate being compared to Nazi nationalists. This presents difficult obstacles for those who consider themselves highly patriotic to honestly appraise their attitudes. Given the touchy nature of the topic, I will make a feeble attempt to lighten up our exposition of nationalism's characteristics by modifying Jeff Foxworthy's well-known "You may be a redneck if . . ." routine. The intent is to provide a context for examining how you can understand the place of country within your own overall worldview.

1. If you believe that God's plan for history would be severely hampered if the United States did not exist in a hundred years, twenty-five years, or even next year, you may be a nationalist. From the earliest settlement of this country by European immigrants, Winthrop's vision of America as a "City upon a Hill" (1630) has had a profound effect on our national self-understanding. In part of his address (with our updated spellings) to his band of settlers, Winthrop says,

> For we must consider that we shall be as a City upon a Hill, the eyes of all people are upon us; so that if we shall deal falsely with our God in this work we have undertaken and so cause him to withdraw his present help from us, we shall be made a story and a byword through the world, we shall open the mouths of enemies to speak evil of the ways of God and all professors for God's sake; we shall shame the faces of many of God's worthy servants, and cause their prayers to be turned into curses upon us until we are consumed out of the good land where we are going.[1]

This concept of America as the heir of God's covenant plan, a New Israel, that the entire world will look to as God's model for all nations is deeply embedded in our national psyche. Similarly, here we find the idea that we will prosper under God's unique protection as long as we remain faithful.

Winthrop's "City upon a Hill" was not content to remain isolated upon the hill for long. It soon became America's "Manifest Destiny" to spread the ideals, and the borders, of the nation from one ocean to another. In the process, the supposed goodness and godliness of our ends

---

[1]See Allen Carder, *Puritan Theology in America: Religion and Life in Seventeenth Century Massachusetts* (Grand Rapids: Baker, 1990), pp. 29-30.

was often used as a nationalistic justification for some pretty coercive means of arriving at this divine destiny. As the physical expansionism of the United States began to wind down toward the middle of the nineteenth century, the idea of America as a chosen nation was increasingly framed in millennial language. In this view, the United States was the fountain from which God's millennial kingdom would stretch across the globe. American missionary and evangelistic impulses would provide the engine, while our political system and principles supplied the heart of the God's kingdom on earth.

Given these links between God's plan and the role of the United States, the idea that this country could cease to exist is unthinkable. However, while many may believe that the "City upon a Hill" has lost some of its sheen, that our Manifest Destiny to expand the physical boundaries has been satisfied, or that postmillennialism should be shelved for some other eschatological model, these views demonstrate that the idea of American exceptionalism can flex with the circumstances. If, therefore, you believe for any reason that God's ultimate plan for all the nations is inextricably bound up with the fate of the United States, you may be a nationalist.

2. If you find it unthinkable that a citizen would not be able to pledge allegiance to the flag or sing the national anthem for religious reasons, you may be a nationalist. It is fashionable in many Christian circles today to be dismissive of long-standing Christian rituals. The word *liturgy* evokes yawns, reciting creeds is viewed as archaic, and the sacraments are treated rather casually. However, when it comes to national rituals, people get pretty fired up. You may remember the recent furor when judicial action questioned the inclusion of the phrase "under God" in the pledge of Allegiance (a phrase which, by the way, was not part of the pledge until 1954). My point is not whether the phrase should or should not be in this pledge (although later I will ask how it should be understood), but whether our attitude toward national rituals tells us something about the alignment, or misalignment, of our loyalties.

Ritual always finds a place in religion, citizenship and football teams because it provides an essential way to express our shared commitments in a community setting. By engaging in ritual, we buy into the group, organization or team. Conversely, then, when we refuse to engage in pledges, salutes or anthems, it appears to be a rejection of such an association. As a result, refusal to place an American flag in the church or participate in our national rituals looks like a failure of patriotism.

This creates a real tension for some Christians, who view pledges of national loyalty as a form of idolatry and in conflict with their allegiance to God. Many times, this grows out of concern about the similarities between patriotic rituals and religious rituals. These parallels, and the fact that the separate obligations to God and country are often combined, lead some Christians to avoid all nationalist rituals. Another factor is historical in nature. Many Christian traditions, perhaps yours, were birthed out of dissent against state-churches. These state-churches frequently responded by convincing the government to persecute, and in some cases execute, members of the dissenting church. Thus, church-state alliances have often led to nations persecuting Christians in the name of Christianity. This danger, in addition to the danger that one's faith can be co-opted or absorbed into our political identity, leads many Christians to avoid all such national ceremonies.

On the one hand, our view is that rituals proclaiming one's place within a national family are not necessarily a violation of our primary commitment to Christ and his church. On the other hand, we are glad that there are Christians who refuse participation in our national rituals. They provide a necessary reminder that the balance between my national allegiance and my commitment to the faith demands constant attention so the two are not confused. If, however, it is unthinkable to you that flags, national anthems or patriotic pledges can attain a sacramental status that rivals, undercuts or co-opts one's Christian allegiance, you may be a nationalist.

3. If you think our Declaration of Independence embodies eternal principles or that the Constitution should never be changed, you may be a nationalist. The sentence above is a bit sneaky since our Constitution, in fact, has been changed by amendment several times. The necessity of doing this should make clear that even good foundational documents do not reach the level of infallibility or perfection, but apparently this is not the case for some. A colleague of ours reported that half of his students in a class (overwhelmingly Christian) put the inspiration of the Declaration of Independence on par with that of Scripture.

As we mentioned earlier, nations often seek to solidify the loyalty of citizens by claiming that their foundations are grounded in eternal truths. For secular nationalism, these unshakable verities are what set them apart from other nations and make them exceptional. It then becomes their mission to disperse these truths, sometimes by force if necessary. Religious nationalism equates political truths with revelation found in holy texts or God's will. The seedbed for such ideas appears in our Declaration of Independence, in which rights of "life, liberty and the pursuit of happiness" are "inalienable rights" precisely because we are endowed with these by our Creator. When this is given a nationalistic twist, then, one's nation becomes the instrument by which this divine message is proclaimed.

Constitutions and other national documents are important guides for political doctrine. However, nationalism comes into existence when political doctrines become dogma and assume a scriptural level of authority. A couple of observations can help guard against the danger of giving such status to political documents. The first is to note that a careful reading of any constitution reveals close parallels with the ideas and circumstances of the age in which it was written. The founding documents of the United States, for example, are strongly shaped by Enlightenment philosophy, an intellectual movement often in profound conflict with Christianity.

The second observation is related. The United States' Constitution has, in our opinion, served this country pretty well for a good stretch of time. At the same time, we have recognized its shortcomings over time. For example, we corrected (by amendment) the idea that "we the people" excluded those who were slaves or female. The point is that, while we honor fundamental documents and ideas of a country, we should combine this with a recognition of the imperfections and time-bound ideas within them. If this sense of humility is absent, you may be well down the road to becoming a nationalist.

4. If you believe that our nation would finally be OK if it would just

get back to "how it was" at some earlier stage of our history, you may be a
nationalist. A couple of decades ago, conservative Christians had a
strong sense of being political and social outsiders. Even with recent
increased political clout, the feeling that evangelicals are on the losing
side of a culture war remains. The exact nature of the cultural problem
is sometimes foggy, but it often includes things like the absence of
prayer or the teaching of evolution in public schools, or the battles over
abortion and gay marriage. The supposed antidote for the nation's ills
is sought by a recovery of some golden age within our national history
when those things did not exist. Usually, this blessed and right time is
not specifically identified, but it often looks a lot like the world the
Cleaver family inhabited.

This is nationalism with a twist because it sees a country's present
state as a departure from God's will. However, the exceptionalism that
forms nationalism's core is present in the idea that the nation once was
the beneficiary of God's unique blessing. Moreover, this blessing can be
regained by a return to the proper interpretation of the Constitution or
the correct cultural norms. In short, then, one's duty as a Christian is
brought into intimate connection with one's duty as a citizen.

Several problems emerge immediately from this idea. First, when
"golden eras" are defined by a narrowly construed set of issues, they
quickly take on a mythical character in which all the blemishes of that
gilded age are ignored or glossed over. Thus, it is common to hear a
desire to return to the Christianity of our founding fathers without
recognizing that many of them were deists who talked a lot about God
but were hostile toward Christianity. A second problem is that we run
the risk of turning God into a vending machine with the idea that he
will provide us with the national protection, status and well-being if we
behave in proper ways. Finally, our return to God's favor is generally
thought to be orchestrated by political actions that will get us back on
the right cultural and moral track. In each case, Christians are tempted
to rely on political methods and goals to define our mission.

Nostalgia in moderate doses is a good thing, because it is a reminder
of all the good we have experienced in the past. Moreover, it is hard to
dispute that some of the things of our past that have disappeared from

the present are sad losses. At the same time, nostalgia always has a mythical tinge to it because it filters out all the negative junk from a bygone period. Nationalistic belief in a "golden era" suffers from the same type of filtration process, so if you believe that God's plan is dependent on removing specific social ills by recovering a piece of the past, you may be a nationalist.

SOME POSITIVE ASPECTS WITHIN NATIONALISM

Nationalism is built around a strong sense of national identity and commitment to one's country, and while a nationalist worldview as a whole is problematic, these two elements have positive aspects. For one thing, they offer a corrective to the individualistic notion that nations are simply a collection of individuals joined together by common assent. In addition to obvious functions, such as providing a legal framework that outlines the rights and responsibilities of citizens and offering protection, nationalism recognizes that a country creates an environment that precedes the individuals within it and shapes their identity. Much of this happens through absorption. However, political stability is also dependent on a citizenry that actively identifies with the history and ideals of the country. It is, therefore, in the best interest of the state to encourage these voluntary commitments, and much positive can result from these displays of patriotism.

1. National identity can help us avoid individualism. One positive aspect of our national allegiances is that they can function as a counterbalance to individualistic and selfish tendencies. Willingness to make sacrifices for something bigger than the individual self is not a natural tendency, but something we must learn. Fulfilling the obligations of citizenship is one of the ways we gain the disciplines associated with unselfishness. Citizenship is also a useful training ground for the virtue of gratitude. While they are always flawed, most nations offer some measure of protection and stability for everyday life, and we have a moral obligation to acknowledge this good through our loyalty.

2. National identity can help overcome narrow tribalism. A common trend today, especially in Western nations, is that populations are becoming more diverse—racially, religiously, linguistically and otherwise.

In this process, we have the opportunity to engage, understand and work with people whose differences might otherwise separate us. Our default tendency is to stay within circles where we feel most comfortable. This frequently leads to stereotyping and prejudices against those who are different in some way. When national ties and duties force us to get beyond these differences, the divisions and biases of tribalism (see chapter eight) can be overcome. In short, life within national boundaries can help erase other boundaries that might keep us apart; common citizenship can provide the context in which we become more aware of the commonalities of human nature. The potential nations provide for helping us discover the common humanity of all, then, is a positive element of our lives within the state.

3. Nations can provide for the common good. History reminds us that life can be insecure and tenuous. We mentioned above that the emergence of the nation-state in recent centuries has been, in large part, an attempt to reduce the risk and insecurity of life by providing a larger entity for the protection and flourishing of citizens. In short, nations offer the scale and size that allow for a measure of protection and economic development not found in smaller social units.

Admittedly, nations have a mixed track record of providing physical protection and preserving even the most basic rights of citizens. Moreover, the additional military power found in the nation-state has often led to empire-building. Despite this spotty background, it is frightening to contemplate what other options hold for us. While the modern nation-state structure holds its own dangers, we can find quite a number of countries around the world that provide for the internal and external defense and work in positive ways to offer educational opportunities, health care and services that advance the well-being of citizens. When this occurs, we should applaud these as positive contributions to human life.

4. National identity can aid us in understanding ourselves. Although generalizations can be misleading and dangerous, we think it is safe to say that Americans, despite our great diversity, tend to be rather individualistic, efficiency-oriented and more pragmatic than theoretically oriented. How did we get there? It is difficult to understand this without knowing something of our history. It will not occur to me why it seems so natural to believe that I have the right to vote for political leaders without consulting a religious or tribal authority, choose my spouse rather than having one assigned to me by my parents, or move fifteen hundred miles away from family apart from some awareness of a legacy provided by my national identity. Much of what we believe to be true, good or just proper manners is not filtered through conscious decision-making processes, but is a matter of absorption. When I recognize that much of what I do and believe has been transmitted through cultural practices, it can act as a reminder that I should be reflective about what I simply accept as truth.

Similarly, awareness of cultural ideas and norms in other countries can challenge my assumptions about the true, the good and the beautiful in healthy ways. For example, when I am around others from cultures that are not as time-obsessed as ours, it forces me to rethink priorities. Where national tradition dictates shutting everything down for the afternoon, I begin to examine my assumptions about how life should be lived. When I become conscious that not all nations have the concept of family that I have assumed to be the norm, I can be more thoughtful about my presuppositions about the structure and place of my own family. In short, greater awareness of differences between cultures can remind us of the relativity of one's own national traditions, ideas and assumptions.

POTENTIAL PROBLEMS WITHIN NATIONALISM

Our overarching critique of a nationalist worldview is that it takes something that is a relative good, and sometimes very good, and transforms it into an absolute good. Viewing one's nation or cultural ideas as supreme is often done unconsciously, and it occurs under a number of conditions that often arise in tandem with each other. At the root of nationalism is a lack of historical perspective, in which we forget the transitory nature of nations and empires. How many empires, imagined in their time to be eternal, are now just faint memories for all but the historian?

This historical blind spot allows us to be seduced by wealth, military power and political influence, which in turn, creates the impression that a nation is doing all the right things and is entitled to that power. Even when nationalists look back on the crumbled and failed empires of the past, they assume that their country is the exception to the rule. In order to make the case for exceptionalism, nationalism frequently wraps religious ideas around the story of the nation. Thus, when "God and country" language are intertwined, one's national culture can be viewed as God's will manifest on earth. Regardless of the particular path taken to nationalism, transforming the relative good of one's nation into the highest good results in a variety of problems.

1. Nationalism transforms that which should be measured into **the standard of measurement.** The belief that our national identity is a relative good implies a duty to constantly revisit, evaluate, and correct our ideas and traditions. Relative goods are always good relative to the standard against which those goods are measured. However, if we lose sight of the final standard against which nations should be judged, we have nothing to reveal their ambiguities and imperfections.

When this happens, our cultural horizon and national traditions become the yardstick by which everything else is measured. The nation that should be subject to judgment becomes, instead, the judge. Energies are directed away from evaluation and improvement, and are oriented toward protecting and maintaining the status quo—whether defined by our history, constitution, superpower status or theological interpretations of national role. Change is therefore seen, not as a potential improvement but as a deviation from the true and the good. Defaulting to the status quo as a benchmark is particularly enticing because our outlook on life is so often absorbed from national and cultural mores rather than consciously chosen. At the same time, since the status quo tends to support our own biases and desires, the result is usually national arrogance.

2. Under nationalism, "the other" is viewed as a challenger. National arrogance is a natural outcome of absolutizing the ideologies of a country. When nationalism draws on its own history, founding documents and rituals as the embodiment of truth against which all others should be judged, other groups will be considered wrong or inferior when any difference is noted. At the very least, this sense of national infallibility eliminates the possibility of using other traditions as backdrops and opportunities for careful reflection on our own political standards. In the worst cases, when outsiders do not conform to our political status quo, nationalism has relegated "the other" to the place of a dangerous challenger that must be defeated. The result has often been horrific bloodshed, usually carried out under the slogan of "God is on our side."

3. Nationalism overreaches in its demand for loyalty. Earlier, we gave due credit to nationalism for recognizing that human beings are inherently social beings and that citizenship is one of the places where we find our identity. In view of this, it is entirely legitimate for our country to seek our loyalty and patriotism. However, nationalism arises when nations stake a greater claim on our loyalties than they deserve. No Christian can offer absolute loyalty to any social structure—nation, family, school, individual church congregation or work—because all are relative goods. Nationalism, however, is a jealous god that does not tolerate relegation of national identity to a position of relative significance. Thus, it plays on our patriotism and legitimate appreciation for the benefits provided by the nation and demands unlimited loyalty, frequently by co-opting religious language and goals for advancing its own agenda. When a nation makes such demands on our commitments, it establishes itself as a competing religion.

4. Nationalism ignores the transnational nature of Christianity. Perhaps one of the most overlooked lessons in Scripture's account of Pentecost (Acts 2) is that Christianity is not the sole possession of any particular nation. Instead, God's new work now transcends old boundaries and encompasses all the nations. Thus, while "Israel" had once applied to a distinctive national/ethnic group, the new "Israel of God" that Paul refers to in Galatians 6:16 refers to a church that erases, among other things, the barriers between Jew and Gentile (Galatians 3:28). The error of religious nationalism is that it attempts to drag Christianity back into the boundaries of a specific nation.

This is where the idea of a Christian nation becomes problematic. While it is indisputable that different nations reflect varying degrees of Christian influence in their histories and present lives, the ideals, mission and means of securing or expressing power are never the same for

Christianity as they are for any nation. Thus, the concept of a Christian nation obscures the fact that the Christian's primary solidarity is not with those who pledge allegiance to a particular flag, but those who confess Jesus as the Lord, regardless of their nationality. The fundamental identity of a Christian is not contained within the documents and history of one's nation, but in the history of God's revelatory work among all peoples. When *Christian* and *nation* are fused, Christianity inevitably takes on a secondary status as the legitimating mechanism for the goals of the state and ceases to be a prophetic voice to the nation.

CONCLUSION

Every group has definite ideas about which worldview is the perpetrator of social evils. Conservative Christians have tended to focus on philosophies like moral relativism as the major culprits of our day. The main reason for this concern is that a philosophy like moral relativism is viewed as an assault on truth, an apprehension we also express in the next chapter. However, in their preoccupation to defend the reality of truth, many Christians have failed to recognize the dangers of worldviews, such as nationalism, that attach themselves to claims of truth. This is a dangerous blind spot. History reveals that far more have suffered and died under nationalism's banner of God and country than under relativism's rallying cry of "whatever." Nationalism has been a violent worldview, and its destructive powers have been energized by its claims to be the bearer of divine goodness and truth. If Christians, who generally resonate very positively with the idea of certainty, want to understand why truth claims cause many to cringe, the ugly history of nationalistic destruction in the name of God's truth sheds light on these concerns. The use of God's name to undergird nationalistic projects is one of the biggest reasons for hostility toward Christianity.

Our intent is not to promote relativism or dismiss the value or goodness of truth. However, declarations of unambiguous truth turn bloody when attached to something as morally and historically ambiguous as nations. It is easy for citizens to overlook our own national moral ambiguities because our social nature compels us to seek our place within the group. Moreover, we want to belong to a winning group.

Those who are insiders within a powerful nation, then, can believe they reside in a New Israel, an idea commonly linked with the United States. However, in the nineteenth century, the slave population commonly referred to the United States not as a New Israel but as the New Egypt. Tragically, many Christians who perceived their nation as the "Promised Land" enslaved other Christians who sought God's deliverance in a new exodus. Those who find a comfortable place within society and, therefore, have a positive bias toward our nation can easily turn a blind eye to faults and imperfections that are clearly seen by those on the outside of power.

Power not only makes it difficult to see our moral shortcomings, but it also obscures our historical ambiguity. Economic well-being and military strength seduce us into believing that a temporary ascendancy is an eternal reality. Every empire has viewed itself as destined by God, or the gods, to rule forever. Every one of them was wrong. A Christian worldview might help explain why. While nationalism seeks a partnership with religion to legitimate its claims, the God of Scripture is not the servant of the nations but their judge. God refuses to be used for political purposes. More strikingly, Scripture makes clear that the most powerful of nations are particularly subject to God's scrutiny and judgment. While nations may have impressive powers, those powers are always temporary and provisional.

The reminder that God refuses to submit to the imperatives of any particular nation reveals that nationalism is really a corporate variation on the sin of pride. Thus, when nationalism speaks of "one nation under God," it proclaims this as a fact rather than a confession that each and every nation is ultimately accountable to God. When nationalism sings "God Bless America," it cannot desire that God would equally bless every other country on earth or understand why God might want to do so. Such prideful attitudes clearly contradict our call to remain humble about our social and political structures.

One of the most difficult tasks of Christianity is learning how to balance the multiple goods that bring benefit to our lives. We count citizenship among the relative goods, and when we learn of atrocities engaged in by other governments, we are grateful for our nation's relative goodness. On the one hand, we are morally bound to give honor and patriotic loyalty to our nation for these benefits. Failure on this count reveals a lack of gratitude. On the other hand, we have a higher moral obligation to qualify and limit our loyalty to relative goods. No nation is the manifestation of absolute goodness. Thus, granting ultimate loyalty to a country indicates that we have lost sight of what is absolutely good and have elevated the nation, a created, transitory and partial good, to a place that should be reserved for God alone.

MORAL RELATIVISM

The Absolute Truth About Relativism and Something Like Relativism

"WE HOLD THESE TRUTHS to be self-evident." This famous first line from the Declaration of Independence introduces some big claims about the political rights of people. However, we may fail to notice that this statement itself represents a significant claim; it asserts that moral and political truths both exist and are knowable. While the eighteenth-century world in which these words were penned generally assumes this, those who offer truth claims today, especially about ethics or politics, seldom get such a pass. Allan Bloom makes the following assessment of university students' beliefs regarding truth. "There is one thing a professor can be absolutely certain of: almost every student entering the university believes, or says he believes that truth is relative."[1]

A seismic shift has indeed occurred in our culture. Many say they no longer believe that truth actually exists, and if it does, it is certainly not self-evident and may not even be knowable. Those who champion the

---

[1]Allan Bloom, *The Closing of the American Mind* (New York: Simon & Schuster, 1987), p. 25.

existence of moral, religious, social or political truth face a barrage of objections about imposing standards on others, intolerance and charges of oppression. In turn, moral relativists are denounced by their opponents as the most serious threat to Christianity, truth and Western civilization. To put it mildly, the question of moral truth is deeply polarizing, with each side looking at the other as *the* major threat to all they hold near and dear. How did we get to this place?

The reality is that we are not really in one particular "place" with relativism but two very different places. Bloom's quote implies this when he states, "almost every student believes, *or says he believes* that truth is relative." We are convinced that the vast majority of people who believe themselves to be moral relativists *say* they are, but are not in reality, moral relativists. Throughout this chapter, we will refer to this position not as moral relativism, but as "moral relativism." If we are correct that "moral relativism" is different from actual moral relativism, most debates across the "moral truth divide" completely miss the point. On the other hand, while they constitute a very small minority, honest-to-goodness moral relativists do exist, so this chapter will address that position as well. In short, then, this chapter addresses two very different things: "moral relativism" and moral relativism. Despite the differences between "moral relativism" and moral relativism, both are rooted in a common impulse. To understand this impulse, we need to take a quick and admittedly overgeneralized survey of key transitions in the genealogy of truth.

A Very Brief History of Truth

By starting with the Declaration of Independence, our chapter breaks in at the middle of truth's history. Ancient thinkers were also very concerned about truth and were generally confident not just that truth existed and could be known but also that it was grounded in the supernatural. Truth's supernatural foundation went by a lot of different names—Logos, the Boundless, the Good, God—but there was strong agreement that truth had a divine anchor. For example, Plato (c. 428-348 B.C.) argues that the most profound realities exist beyond the physical world in a realm he calls the "world of being." The world of being contains realities that are nonphysical, unchangeable and perfect; Plato refers to them as Forms. The highest of these is a divine entity called the Form of the Good. What we experience in our physical reality is, at best, the shadow of the Forms. Because physical objects, which we know by our limited physical senses, are changeable and imperfect, they give us a fuzzy and distorted picture of truth. Our most direct access to the Forms, and truth, comes through reason. While other philosophers during this age relied more heavily on the senses, the majority agreed that truth could only be gleaned from sensation after its data had been processed by the rational mind. Rationality provides the route to truth because the divine is also rational.

As the classical period died and Christian thinkers became the main intellectual engine in the medieval period, they retained the idea that truth was rooted in the spiritual realm. Plato's unchanging "Good" seemed very much like the immutable and perfect Christian God, and Plato's Forms were now understood as the perfect and true realities that radiate from the mind of God. These divine truths are revealed by God through Scripture. At the same time, since God is a rational being, truth were also accessible through reason, although rationality always had to be checked against Scripture. Over the medieval period, the idea that the church and its traditions provided the proper interpretation of this supernatural truth was a central doctrine.

The shift from the medieval world to a modern worldview is complex, but a key catalyst is a deep corruption within the church that undermined its authority as the guardian and arbiter of truth. One reaction to this corruption was the Reformation led by Martin Luther (1483-1546). Among other things, Luther challenged the church's claim to be the ultimate interpreter of Scripture and, by extension, truth. In place of the institutional church, he established the idea of a priesthood of all believers in which each Christian possessed the ability and responsibility to rightly interpret Scripture. This radically democratized, and individualized, access to the truth.

Luther still maintained that truth originated from a divine source (God, revealed through Scripture). However, instead of claiming that truth was filtered through a second, external source (the church), Luther entrusted apprehension of truth to the individual (although he would quickly have added that individual Christians are guided by the Holy Spirit). This new model subtly shifted attention away from the question "What is real/true?" and placed the focus on "How do *I know* what is real/true?"

Descartes (1596-1650), commonly referred to as the "Father of Modern Philosophy," took this shift a step farther. He rejected the idea that we should immediately accept truth as interpreted and propagated through any external source. Instead, Descartes resolved to doubt everything until he found ideas that were utterly beyond doubt. In fact, the first certainty he discovered resulted from his doubting process. Doubting is a form of thinking and thinking requires a thinker. He famously concluded, then, "I think, therefore, I am."

Descartes's conclusion that he existed hardly qualified as a radical departure from widely-held premodern ideas, nor do any of the ideas he deduced from it—that God exists, a physical world exists and that the body and the soul are different things with different characteristics. What was radical, however, was Descartes's method of arriving at these truths. He no longer relied on God, church tradition, Scripture or the accepted truths of the classical philosophers as the starting point for discerning truth. The finite, autonomous and rational individual was now the arbiter of what is real and true.

Descartes and most other modernists were confident that truth existed and could be discovered by reason, but a pitched battle soon followed about how reason actually works. As the modern period progressed, Descartes's deductive method, which placed little trust the senses, fell out of favor. What replaced it was a more inductive approach, which invested faith in claims about things that are observable and subject to quantifiable measures. As a result, many of the Enlightenment's grandchildren retained the belief that truth was attainable, but constricted the category of truth to what we can observe. Thus, statements about unobservable realities such as souls, God and ethics are inadmissible as truth claims, but are reclassified as statements of preference or taste. Thus, a statement such as, "Using torture to obtain potentially useful information from enemy combatants is morally evil," really means, "I don't really like it when people are tortured." It is not, however, a factual claim because evil cannot be observed through a microscope or weighed on a scale.

While modernism narrows the category of truth to the tangible realm, as we move toward what is broadly called postmodernism, the concept of truth further evaporates when many begin to question whether even statements about observable realities are (or can be) free from our biases. Modernism assumed that we could be objective and neutral in our claims about the physical world. Thus, it agreed that a single unifying and knowable reality existed and functioned as the standard for testing truth claims, so long as these claims were statements about the physical world. Postmodernism, however, is suspicious of claims to neutrality in any realm. Consequently, it questions the concept of a unified and knowable body of truth.

Perhaps the best-known proponent of such as view is Friedrich Nietzsche (1844-1900), who believed that truth claims are based solely on each individual's perspective and interpretation. Moreover, these interpretations are not oriented toward attaining truth. Instead, what we call truth is simply a means by which we pursue power. In short, whatever supports our individual biases and helps us accumulate power is labeled truth. Two important ideas grow out of this. First, we cannot universalize any particular interpretation of reality. If bin Laden's agenda supports ours, he is a hero; if not, he is a terrorist. Truth is relative to the interests and projects of the person claiming truth. More importantly, if "truth" is nothing more than the means to gain power over others, truth claims must be viewed as oppressive.

To be sure, not all that is labeled as postmodernism holds such a radical denial of truth as Nietzsche's version. Many forms do not reject truth altogether, but question modernist approaches to our definitions of truth. Nevertheless, as skepticism about our ability to know truth moved from academia to the streets where you and I live, the idea became widespread that truth claims, especially those concerning ethical matters, are presumptuous and dangerous.

"MORAL RELATIVISM" AND MORAL RELATIVISM

It is not hard to see how such a cultural mood created by postmodernism provides a fertile context for moral relativism. Moreover, since moral relativism is frequently viewed as a direct assault on something as basic as truth, it is no surprise that the backlash against it is fierce. This is the context for the so-called culture war. On one side are those who embrace truth as knowable and absolute; on the other side are the relativists. It sounds black and white, but wars of any kind are rarely as simple as they appear on the surface. With a bit of investigation, we find that relativism and absolutism both come in a variety of flavors.

First, it should be noted that even those who claim to be absolutists are really comfortably relativistic in certain areas. For example, any married person is keenly aware that people have different views about the ideal color for a car. Most agree that it is not a big deal if someone favors biking over swimming or potato chips over chocolate cake. People vary in preferences about matters of taste and usually have little problem accepting that these are relative to the individual. While we may not share the same tastes as another, discussions of these differences seem to fall safely outside the category of truth, although some people will certainly make it their business to tell you how wrong you are about your tastes.

Similarly, many who claim to be relativists qualify their relativism. While they may think that the question of capital punishment's permissibility is subjective, they may simultaneously believe that objective, factual means exist for determining whether bikers are more susceptible to knee injury than swimmers or whether potato chips have more calories per ounce than cake. The point is that people are rarely across-the-board subjectivists or objectivists. The real disagreement here, then, isn't whether truth exists. It's really a debate about where we draw the line that separates matters of fact from issues of opinion or taste.

Moral relativists fit here because they limit relativism to the area of ethics (and usually include aesthetics, questions of beauty, in this category as well). Those who put morality on the "opinion" side of the line generally do so because moral issues seem incompatible with observation and quantification. They allow that we can make factual statements about how many times a particular form of abortion is performed and the incidence of physical side-effects, but argue that the moral permissibility of abortion is opinion since good and evil cannot be directly observed or measured.

This approach may fit well with our culture's attraction to "I shouldn't believe it if I can't see it." However, it involves a big assumption about what should be classified as truth. If only claims about what is accessible to the senses and can be measured fit through this filter, religious or moral statements such as "God exists and is a morally good Being" must be dismissed out of hand. Obviously, this assumption needs to be scrutinized. For now, however, a simple observation will suffice: while some provide philosophical reasons for accepting only the observable and measurable as true, the majority simply assume it is true. This sets the stage for our next critical distinction.

While moral relativists sometimes have philosophical reasons for their position, the second type of relativism, which we have labeled "moral relativism," is very different. "Moral relativists" rarely offer reasons for their position. Instead, they give reasons why they are *not* absolutists or legalists. In short, "moral relativists" are, in reality, antilegalists or anti-absolutists. Legalism, in its broadest definition, says that moral truth is contained in laws that should direct our behaviors. "Moral relativism" finds legalistic truth claims distasteful and reacts by embracing relativism as an alternative. If we are correct about this, Christians who function in a legalistic manner are a major cause of "moral relativism," which is ironic because such folks tend to think they are the solution to relativism.

It is not hard to understand "relativism's" reaction against legalism; you may have had the same response. Laws feel cold and impersonal, and they don't care about unique circumstances with real people behind them. As a result, legalists who are keen on making sure the laws are followed often seem unconcerned about the people to whom the rules are applied. Additionally, laws are generally framed in negative language; they tell us what we *should not* do. Few people have a positive response to prohibitions or to the people who make it their duty to remind us of them, so the impulse to react against legalism is understandable. Laws also have a hard edge; they present themselves as settled truth, not as discussion points. A conviction on the charge of grand theft auto is not an invitation to debate the merits of personal property rights. The law against auto theft is there, and it isn't budging. Legalists don't budge on their moral laws either. They have the moral truth and that is what is important to them.

We have all seen how this plays out. Someone acts in a way that a legalist perceives as an offense to moral law (and often is). The legalist calls them on it in a way that seems (and often is) arrogant, intolerant or impersonal. The first person finds this annoying, rejects the arrogance and intolerance reflected in the legalist's truth claims and argues that each person is free to derive their own personal moral standards. In short, they adopt "moral relativism," believing that it is moral relativism. The legalist perceives this as a total rejection of moral truth, becomes more anti-"moral relativist," and asserts the laws more forcefully. Of course, the stronger the assertion of these laws, the more the "moral relativist" is reinforced in his or her position.

THE CASE FOR MORAL RELATIVISM

Just as there are different forms of relativism, the reasons people adopt a relativistic approach also vary widely. Since "relativism" is primarily reactionary, the reasons for adopting it are emotional rather than intellectual. We will examine these first, and then consider three intellectual foundations for philosophical forms of relativism.

One emotional appeal to "moral relativism" is that it resonates with our desire to treat people kindly. Legalism can be very harsh because it seems to take pleasure in telling other people how wrong they are. Since most of us want to be nice (or at least want others to think we are nice), "moral relativism" appears to offer an easy way to avoid meanness. If all actions are morally equal, we never have to ever tell anyone they are wrong. Second, some embrace "relativism" for selfish reasons. We all occasionally do things that bring the disapproval of others. "Relativism" offers a way to justify such actions by claiming that ethical standards are personal. When someone disapproves of our behavior, "relativism" makes it their problem because they have imposed their individual standard on us. Finally, many adopt "relativism" out of intellectual laziness. If one stakes out an ethical position on any topic, the assumption is that you have to defend it. Quite frankly, defending ideas is hard work. "Relativism" takes the easy way out because it creates the illusion that we don't have to do the heavy lifting of supporting our ideas.

The last two reasons—selfishness and laziness—don't provide a compelling motivation for shaping an aspect of our lives as important as ethics, so they don't need much comment. Concerning the first motivation, the desire to be nice to others is commendable. In fact, we like it when people are nice. However, relativism is a kinder and gentler type of ethics *only if* there is no objective moral truth. If all moral ideas are equal, then we have no business telling others they are wrong. However, *if* moral truth has an objective reality and makes a real difference in one's quality of life, it would not be nice to let people wreck their lives by acting on error. In short, then, we cannot decide whether moral relativism is nicer than moral objectivism until we determine which is true. Thus, we need to examine philosophical reasons for advocating moral relativism.

The first argument for moral relativism presents it as a natural outgrowth of *atheism*. Briefly stated, this position argues that any objective and universal truth must be anchored in a transcendent reality such as God. If there is no God, we have no foundation for truth of any kind, moral truth included. In short, it asserts that Dostoyevsky was correct in his claim that everything is permissible if God does not exist.

A second intellectual basis for moral relativism highlights what philosophers call an *epistemological* (knowing) problem. The epistemological problem reminds us of the difference between something's reality and our knowledge of that reality. For example, as long as I've been around, Mt. Everest has been the highest point on our planet. For several years of my life, however, I was unaware of this reality, even though my ignorance did not change that reality. The epistemological argument says that, while clear methods exist for determining the highest elevation on earth, the same may not be the case for determining what is ethically true, even if ethical truth does exist.

The reasons for this uncertainty vary. Some highlight, as we have seen above, the problem of getting beyond individual or cultural biases to think and see in a neutral and clear manner. Others focus on the inadequacy of language to bridge the gap between the person who seeks to know and whatever it is that we might know. In any case, this argument recognizes that it is extremely difficult to make a case for any moral truth that is not open to criticism and counterargument. Many conclude, then, that if a definitive defense for our moral conclusions is not available, we are left to our own resources. Our opinions become the final court of appeal because, while we cannot be certain of any moral realities, we can be sure of our preferences.

The third foundation for moral relativism comes from the Sophist philosopher, Protagoras (c. 490-420 B.C.), who stated that "each person is the measure of truth." Protagoras's final criterion for truth was *individual perception*. This position takes the bold step of removing the line between "I perceive" and "I know." To have a sense perception is the same as knowing. This has significant ramifications. First, since each individual perceives things differently, it follows logically that individuals with different perceptions know different truths. Second, our perceptions are what they are. What we see, hear, feel, taste or smell is not a matter of choice. We cannot change them nor, for that matter, can anyone else. A third factor is that our perceptions are private. It therefore makes little sense for another person to argue that our reports about perception are wrong, because no one else perceives our perceptions. We might lie about what we have seen, but no other person is in a position to tell us what we actually did see. If all this is true, then it seems that the moral conclusions we draw from perceptions cannot be challenged by others. We are morally infallible.

Whether one comes at relativism from the direction of atheism, the difficulty of moral certainty or the individual nature of perception, the conclusions are similar. The first is that no one has access to any sort of universal moral truth. That leaves moral evaluation up to each individual's perceptions or preferences, which makes it illegitimate for me to judge another's views by my own conclusions. It would be similarly wrong for others to evaluate my moral beliefs or actions by their individual standards.

To make such judgments without a universal standard of truth, then, is to impose one's truth on another person. It is something like forcing a soccer player to play by the rules of a kindergarten classroom, which usually requires that students refrain from running, yelling or kicking. These rules, beneficial in a kindergarten setting, impose severe limitations on a soccer player (although most soccer referees would probably appreciate less yelling). Various words could be used to describe what would happen in such a situation. We could say that it is arrogant and intolerant to suppose that kindergarten classroom standards are so universal, absolute and true that they should be applied to soccer players. We could say that applying rules so alien to the basics of soccer does violence to that game. We could say that kindergarten class rules are harsh restrictions on the freedom of soccer players. In the same way, moral relativism argues that imposing one's truths on another person is arrogant, intolerant, violent and freedom-robbing. Relativism's alternative, therefore, is to promote a humble, peaceful tolerance that allows each person to freely pursue and express individual truth.

POSITIVE ELEMENTS WITHIN MORAL RELATIVISM

1. Moral relativism helps us recognize moral selectivity. As you survey the aims of moral relativism at the end of the previous paragraph, you probably will not find much to disagree with. Who shouldn't want to promote peace, freedom, humility and tolerance? We could have lively discussions about what lengths we should go to keep peace, the limits of individual freedom, where we cross the line between true humility and becoming a doormat, or what we should tolerate, but moral relativism seems to be on the right track when it promotes these as general moral principles.

The fact that moral relativism does advocate moral principles such as peacefulness and humility creates interesting problems for relativism, as we will see later on, but it also reveals a common blind spot for those who favor absolutist approaches to ethics—selectivity. Folks on the absolutist side of the moral spectrum are very concerned about getting their moral principles *right*, but they often fail to ask whether they get *all* of them.

This was illustrated for me when I had a guest speaker talk to a class about themes in the Gospels. He pointed out that Christians often emphasize certain moral issues that Scripture mentions infrequently but overlook other moral concerns found on about every page of the Bible. Thus, moral absolutists often fixate, for example, on issues such as divorce, abortion, euthanasia and homosexuality, matters that are rarely addressed directly in the Bible, but they read right past the hundreds of passages that directly call us to care for the poor.

Our point is not that we should gauge the importance of moral issues by how frequently they are mentioned in Scripture. Instead, the illustration should make us aware of our selectivity about which moral principles we adopt as *our* pet issues. I would argue that part of the popularity of "moral relativism" is its attempt to recover many of the virtues (such as peace, freedom, moral humility and tolerance) present in Scripture that we have filtered out through selectivity. Thus, "moral relativists" want Christians to recognize the incompatibility of hurling rocks at people heading for abortion clinics. To be fair, moral relativism is equally guilty of its own sort of selectivity about which moral qualities it emphasizes. Too often the choice has been framed as an either-or decision—either we choose the values advocated by those who believe in objective moral truth or we focus on those championed by moral relativists. This is a false dilemma. Nevertheless, moral relativism provides valuable assistance to nonrelativists by helping them recognize selectivity in establishing their moral agendas and where they have imposed those agendas on Scripture rather than getting their agendas from Scripture itself.

2. Moral relativism illuminates the inadequacy of legalism. While the previous section focuses on the tendency to be selective about *which* moral principles we use, we should also give attention to *how* moral principles are used. Dallas Willard, a philosopher and prominent author, tells about a time in a graduate seminar when he offered his opinion that divorce is always wrong. Years later, he recounts,

> I came across the situation of a devout woman whose husband had married her as a cover for his homosexuality. He consummated the marriage so it couldn't be annulled, and after that he had nothing to do with her. They had no personal relationship at all. He would bring his male friends home and, in her presence, have sex in the living room or wherever else they pleased. Her religious guides continued to tell her that she must stay in "the marriage," while she died a further death every day, year after year.[2]

---

[2]Dallas Willard, *The Divine Conspiracy: Rediscovering Our Hidden Life in God* (New York: Harper-One, 1998), p. 173.

Through the unjust pain endured by this woman, Willard concluded that divorce is permissible under certain circumstances. This does not mean that Willard has totally disregarded moral rules and lapsed into moral relativism. Instead, this conclusion recognizes that no moral rule, regardless of how true or good, is an end in itself. When rules displace the physical safety or spiritual well-being of real human beings in tragic situations as our first concern, we have become legalistic.

The coldness of legalistic uses of ethical principles is what drives many toward "moral relativism." We believe these "moral relativists" go off track when they conclude that the only solution for legalism is the rejection of moral rules altogether. However, they are correct to conclude that something is seriously wrong when rules take priority over hurting people. To this extent, then, moral relativism can help us recognize that even good ethical principles can become tools of oppression when applied legalistically.

3. Moral relativism forces us to be more reflective about ethical positions and methods. It would not be surprising to discover that some readers will conclude that Willard's position on the divorce case above was wrong. The fact is that *any* decision *anyone* might make about *any* moral question will draw fire from some direction. For better or worse, there is little consensus today on what constitutes right and wrong. On the surface, these challenges appear to reflect a moral relativism. Notice, however, that when people challenge certain traditional ideas about the morality of divorce, embryonic stem-cell research, abortion or myriad other issues, they base their objections on moral virtues such as a desire for healing or freedom of choice, moral ideas they (correctly) assume should be accepted by all. Thus, for all the bluster from those who believe themselves to be relativists, their position is not whether objective and universal moral standards exist, but whether certain traditional moral ideas correctly interpret how we should apply or prioritize these moral standards. In other words, such folks are "moral relativists," not moral relativists.

This questioning of previously accepted ethical views is frequently viewed as a dangerous thing, and these queries do carry risks. At the same time, failure to question widely accepted moral ideas is similarly

risky. First, unless we challenge traditional beliefs, we may simply perpetuate bad ideas if the traditional beliefs are wrong. Belief in the moral
goodness of slavery or the concept of women as property was once
deeply embedded in tradition, but most agree that reevaluation and
elimination of these practices was a positive move. Second, even when
traditional beliefs have validity, they are often asserted without any explanation as to why they are wise paths to follow. This, we believe, accounts for much of the current rebellion against older moral views—we
have done a poor job of showing why they became broadly held in the
first place (and we may have forgotten ourselves). Finally, moral positions we struggle with and embrace voluntarily are more deeply integrated into our lives than those we simply absorb by osmosis. Carefully
considering the claims of alternatives can be an important step in gaining ownership of our ethical conclusions. On balance, then, moral relativism's skeptical attitude toward moral truth, or at least traditionally
held moral views, should be viewed as a positive opportunity to
reexamine our ethical assumptions and foundations.

POTENTIAL PROBLEMS WITHIN MORAL RELATIVISM

We have stated that many who claim to be moral relativists are, in reality, "moral relativists" reacting against a moral perspective they don't
want to embrace (usually a form of legalism). Nevertheless, some folks
do have a philosophical commitment to relativism that needs to be addressed. We will begin with a brief inquiry into the philosophical problems with moral relativism, but will also focus our attention on the
practical and moral difficulties that generally address the perspective of
"moral relativism."

   1. How does one make an intellectual case for moral relativism?
Many gravitate toward moral relativism because no argument that
moral truths are objective and rooted in something eternal is universally accepted as conclusive proof. In fact, probably the majority of
people who embrace objective moral truth admit that while they can
frame a coherent case for it, they cannot prove their position. However, it must also be said that the inability to prove the existence of
moral truth does not make the opposite position—the absence of

moral truth—true by default. Moral relativism also has the duty to make a coherent case for its position.

Shaping a coherent intellectual argument for moral relativism is particularly tricky since many relativists do not discount just the existence of moral truth but truth in general. At the most fundamental level, the question is how one can argue that relativism is *true* if it tosses out the entire category of truth from the beginning. To claim that it is universally true that no universal truth exists sounds a bit suspect. Moreover, most relativists do not limit themselves to claiming that relativism in general is true. They also argue that specific things are true. For example, relativism asserts that, if there is no objective moral truth, we should tolerate ethical ideas that vary from our own.

Three observations seem to follow naturally from this. First, it is hard to know how one can demand tolerance unless we believe that tolerance is a moral requirement for everyone. In other words, this makes tolerance a moral absolute. But doesn't relativism reject moral absolutes? On the other hand, to require tolerance on the basis of individual preference appears to be the epitome of intolerance. Either way, it is not clear how relativism escapes glaring inconsistency on this count.

Second, the idea that we should be tolerant does not function as just any sort of truth, but it is framed as a moral truth. From the relativist perspective, an intolerant person is not simply out of synch with a differing opinion. People who are intolerant are bad—morally bad. However, if no objective standard exists for making such moral judgments about people and their activities, no matter how intolerant they are, how can such an evaluation be justified?

The third problem is something of the flip-side of the last. Tolerant people are thought to be morally good people. However, if whatever another person is doing is good (so long as they are not acting in an intolerant manner), why do we have to *tolerate* certain behaviors? If I believe an act is good, I don't simply tolerate it; I enjoy and celebrate it. The idea that we have to tolerate the behaviors and ideas of others either implies that (a) we believe they are wrong or (b) that our evaluations about what they are up to are wrong (since we only tolerate something that is, in reality, good). The former seems to be contradictory since moral relativism has no universal basis to judge an act as wrong, and the latter contradicts relativism's view that one's own moral views are infallible. In short, the entire concept of tolerance assumes that certain actions are wrong.

The very goodness of the ideas that make moral relativism attractive to many—peace, humility, freedom and tolerance—creates a problem for moral relativism. Moral relativism does not promote these principles as mere individual values that someone can embrace or reject. Instead, they function as universal moral goods, the very thing that moral relativism denies. Thus, moral relativism attempts to ground itself in the very thing it claims to reject.

2. No one can live as a relativist. As difficult as it is to coherently wrap our minds around relativism, it is even more complicated to live consistently within the fundamental axioms of this worldview. For example, what would happen if a committed relativist was randomly selected for abduction and torture? No doubt, the tortured relativist will think that the torturers are doing something wrong. However, the torturers might use the relativist's own argument as justification for their actions. There are, after all, varying opinions about the moral status of torture, and each opinion has equal moral authority. Given the circumstances, our hypothetical relativist will have a difficult time accepting such reasoning. No one really acts as if ethics is a matter of opinion when they fall victim to actions they consider wrong.

The example above tells us something rather obvious; no one actually tolerates everything. It is not hard to understand why. Try to envision a world in which all external constraints on human behavior are removed. Of course, rules and laws about honesty, protection of human life and health, when and how people can be deprived of freedoms, and security for property would all be discarded. After all, laws are external standards. Now that we have removed these laws and set everyone free to act according to their individual preferences, what happens next? It's not hard to imagine that such a world would be quite chaotic. Would we be obligated to tolerate everything that would occur in such a world?

Actually, ancient philosophers who embraced relativism acknowledged the "chaos factor" of this worldview, and they split on how we should respond. One response proposed by Callicles (Protagoras's fellow Sophist) says that when we get rid of truth, all that is left is power. This leads logically to a "might makes right" approach in which all do their best to claw their way to power and then do whatever is necessary to hang on to it. In other words, forget tolerance. Our job is to create the world according to our *individual self-interest.*

The second option is offered by Protagoras. He argued that, in the absence of truth, we simply negotiate ways to live together peacefully. We replace the old rules based on external authority with new ones constructed from compromises made out of *mutual self-interest.* We should not pretend, however, that these negotiated social rules are really true. They are merely agreements that allow us to escape the intolerable results of social chaos.

Which way of living makes sense for a relativist? Logically, Callicles' solution is more consistent. If no objective truth exists, what do we really gain if we immediately create our own pretend truth with rules that limit our individual self-interest, as Protagoras proposed? Moreover, Protagoras's solution implies that order is better than anarchy. But how, given relativism's elimination of truth, can we make a value judgment about the superiority of peace to chaos? At the same time, no one who has a choice really wants to live in, or tolerate, Callicles' "dog-eat-dog" world, and very few ultimately survive such a world. The practical reality is that rules, laws and guidelines are indications of the limits of our tolerance. This in itself does not necessarily prove that such rules are objectively true, but it reminds us that the elimination of all rules in favor of individual preferences is impossible in practice.

3. Moral relativism undercuts the principles of fairness and justice. The options presented by Protagoras and Callicles help us recognize another problem with moral relativism—it completely undermines the concept of justice. Our everyday language is sprinkled with references to justice. If you have children, you can't make it an hour without hearing, "That's not fair." With moral relativism's individualistic standard of ethics, what do we do with language about justice and fairness? Both words assume what relativism rejects—an external standard of right or wrong. If one believes, as moral relativists do, that justice is an individual concept and that one person's justice is another's injustice, we are left with two options. Differing parties can remain entrenched in their opposing concepts of fairness until one forces the other to accept his or her view (Callicles' position). In other words, this option carries moral relativism to its logical conclusion and replaces justice with power.

The second option is that we negotiate some agreement about what constitutes fairness (Protagoras's option). The problems with this are numerous (for example, if we are morally infallible, why would we compromise our idea of moral truth?), but we will focus on one ramification of this position. If justice is whatever we can get all parties to agree on, we must acknowledge that justice is arbitrary. We make it up as we go. This may seem fine until we consider what we expect justice to do for us. It is the basis for determining when and how we will require people to give up some of their private property for the common good (taxation), the conditions under which we will deprive people of their freedom through imprisonment, or when it is permissible to end someone's life. If justice is nothing but an arbitrary agreement reached through negotiation, the implications are huge. We could sentence someone to life imprisonment for planting tomatoes and give people a tax credit for committing murder. Hitler could be afforded the same moral status as Mother Teresa. Without external standards, nothing prohibits such mutually brokered rules or moral evaluations.

4. *Moral relativism results in the lowest common moral denominator.* Moral relativism is, at best, a minimalist approach to ethics. It only offers guidance on what we *cannot* do, but it cannot tell us what we *should* do. At first glance, this does not seem to be the case. After all, doesn't moral relativism say that we are permitted to do anything, or almost anything, we want? Here's the problem. Moral relativism *permits* anything—it tells us what is allowable—but it cannot tell us what we *should* do or be. Some variations on relativism tell us what we *should not* do (e.g., we should not harm others or be intolerant). In this way, it can keep us from being evil. However, avoiding evil is not the same as being morally good, nor is doing what is allowable the same as goodness. Ironically, then, moral relativism falls into the same problem of legalistic approaches to ethics. Both legalism and moral relativism set up rules that define what we should avoid in order to stay away from evil. However, neither legalism nor moral relativism can tell us how to be *good*. Such minimalist views are a far cry from what is necessary to guide us toward moral excellence.

CONCLUSION

As a satisfying worldview, moral relativism fails on multiple levels. It can't make an intellectual case for itself without reverting to the idea of truth, a category it denies from the outset. Moreover, without a substructure of external truth, relativism's universal demand for tolerance and freedom has nothing to support it. If moral truths are radically individual and infallible, we have no basis to dispute individuals who believe that suicide bombers are models of virtue. Cries for justice are transformed into power games or reduced to individual pleadings grounded in nothing but personal preference. Moral relativism tells us not to harm another person, but it has no foundation for requiring that we help others. It demands tolerance, but the moral distance between merely tolerating others and loving them is vast. Thus, when relativism replaces moral goodness with a minimalist ethics of toleration, it provides no adequate vision of what a good person is.

All of the points above seem to offer solid fundamental reasons to reject moral relativism. At the same time, our argument in this chapter is that the more widespread issue is "moral relativism," not moral relativism. The causes for "moral relativism" are not primarily intellectual, so the arguments offered above don't help us make much headway against this variation. Instead, since "moral relativism" is primarily a reaction, we cannot really address it unless we know what it is reacting to and against. This is where I think Christians need to pay close attention, because, as stated above, I believe we have been a major cause of "moral relativism." And if we find "moral relativism" problematic, we need to listen closely to what its advocates say if we are going to offer a solution. Here are four suggestions for ways to counter "moral relativism."

1. Admit that we are not God. Some readers have probably noted that the terms "absolutes" and "absolute truth" have not been used much in this chapter. Christians deeply engaged in the "culture war" against moral relativism will find this puzzling, since many believe that moral absolutes are the chief weapon in their arsenal. I have no problem saying that moral absolutes exist. This seems to follow naturally from the Christian understanding of God's nature. If God is both absolute and moral, the moral standards that emanate from his nature are as well. However, the statement that moral absolutes *exist* is a very different one than the claim that *I know* these absolutes with the same clarity that God knows them. Absolute truth is not the same thing as absolute knowing. When Christians claim to have a "God's-eye view" that grants them absolute moral knowledge, many folks become so annoyed that they abandon the idea of moral absolutes and, in doing so, believe themselves to be moral relativists.

2. Get the real issues straight. If the existence of moral absolutes is different from the issue of how clearly we know these absolutes, the second suggestion follows logically from the first. Christians do not have a monopoly on the desire to be ethical, so we need to quit acting like we do. Once we acknowledge this, we can get beyond the silly assumption that "moral relativists" do not take ethics seriously. The real issues center on the question of which moral principles are fundamental, how we know moral truth and how we should apply that truth to actual circumstances. If both Christians and "moral relativists" recognize that the disagreements arise in these areas, discussions take a more productive tone. When Christians fail to recognize that "moral relativists" care deeply about moral truth, we only alienate them.

3. Be a little more humble about ethical issues. If "moral relativists" want Christians to hear anything, I'm convinced it is this: The answers to many ethical questions are not always obvious and clear-cut. Christians often assume that they are deficient if they do not have a ready answer for every moral question that arises. As a result, we give the impression that we don't think carefully about complex issues and, instead, rely on high-profile leaders to provide all the "right" answers. And I think this suspicion is often justified. When it comes to any ethical issue—immigration law, divorce, economic justice, stem-cell research and myriad other hot topics—we need to admit that we are dealing with complicated issues that have real flesh-and-blood people attached to them. This doesn't mean that we should not take a stand on these questions; true humility does not require that we abandon our commitments or beliefs. However, humility does require that we be informed, ready to admit that those who disagree also have moral motives behind their positions and that we should listen carefully to opponents because we, who are not God, may be wrong.

4. Think of absolutes in terms of character rather than actions. Finally, let us return to the question of absolutes. I think that the idea of moral absolutes is very helpful if we think of it primarily in terms of character. In other words, we should absolutely be just, compassionate, loving and *tolerant*. Many will find the last characteristic surprising because champions of moral truth frequently throw out the "toleration baby" with the "relativistic bath water." However, moral relativism, by throwing out universal moral virtues, has no foundation for prescribing tolerance. In addition, the fact that God gives human beings the ability to make choices, and allows us to choose in ways that run counter to his will, seems to show that tolerance has a place in God's nature. This tolerance certainly has limits, but it seems clear that he permits actions that he disagrees with.

In any case, if we think of moral absolutes as moral qualities rather than specific actions, this grounds our fundamental ethical impulse in God's own nature. It also makes us aware that even when I know that I have an absolute moral obligation to be just, compassionate and tolerant toward illegal immigrants, I may not have clear answers about what actions are required to properly apply these absolutes. Finally, when people disagree with me about ethical matters, this approach requires that I still respect their ethical impulses.

This is admittedly only a starting point, but if Christians would do this much, we believe that many of the problems of "moral relativism" dissolve. In the end, however, what we have suggested above is not just a strategy. Instead, it seems to be consistent with the type of moral character Christians need for navigating the moral tangles of a fallen world.

SCIENTIFIC NATURALISM

Only Matter Matters

A{T ONE POINT IN THE MOVIE} *Awakenings* Robin Williams's character, a neurologist named Dr. Malcolm Sayer, points to the Periodic Table of Elements and says, "It's the universe at its essence. You see, you have your alkaline metals; you have your halogens, your inert gases. Every element has its place in that order. You can't change that. It's secure no matter what."

Dr. Sayer's words provide a nice summary of naturalism. Naturalism, sometimes also called reductive physicalism, scientism, scientific naturalism or materialism (although Madonna used the term in a different manner), holds that all that exists is physical and can be reduced to its elemental material composition. These elements are, as Dr. Sayer says, "the universe at its essence." *Essence* refers to what something really is after you have stripped away all the superficial properties and characteristics. When scientific naturalism speaks of this essence, it uses a wide variety of terms to describe the fundamental components of reality—atoms, elements, energy or something else. Regardless of which term or idea provides the most accurate description, this essence manifests itself in and as matter, the physical stuff of which the universe is comprised. The category of matter includes a lot of things—park benches, asteroids, manatees and human beings—but it is also noticeable for what it excludes. If nothing exists except the material, there are no nonphysical entities such as God or souls.

Eliminating God from the picture requires a radical redefinition of the universe. If nonphysical realities do not exist, no room is left for either a personal Creator or an impersonal force that brings forth something from nothing. In naturalism, the physical matter of which the universe consists is eternal. In this worldview, then, creation is not the emergence of something out of nothing. At most, when a naturalist speaks of creation, it refers to the eternal raw materials undergoing a continual process of change. Thus, it might be possible to say that the universe did not exist at some time billions of years in the past because matter was not then arranged in a manner that would be recognizable as "the universe." Nevertheless, the basic realities (the essences) have always been around. The world is a closed system. Nothing essentially new comes into existence; nothing in existence disappears in this closed system. The fundamental components of which the universe consists simply go through a perpetual process of reconfiguration. It's a bit like committee work.

If the eternal materials of the universe are caught up in a never-ending dance of reconfiguration, a natural question to ask is what is driving and directing this change. For naturalism, everything that happens in the cosmos is governed by what we refer to frequently as the "laws of nature." As soon as we speak of these laws of nature, we run into the same kind of problem we encounter with matter. Naturalism finds it difficult to say what these laws actually are. In fact, they present a unique problem to naturalism's idea that everything is material, since no one thinks of these laws as physical entities. Some naturalists therefore speak of these laws, not as things, but as necessary or useful hypotheses. Of course, this approach is somewhat awkward since it makes naturalism's entire worldview dependent on hypothetical entities that do not meet their own criteria for reality.

In any case, these laws, whatever they are, are presumed by naturalism to have two particularly important characteristics. First, the laws of nature are not seen as intentionally created entities. In many popular forms of naturalism, they are thought to be eternal. More recent cosmologies, however, view these laws as emerging in the very first moments following the big bang and, thus, virtually as old as the universe, though not strictly eternal. In any case, the laws of nature are not thought to have originated in a purposeful act of creation. Nor are they themselves understood as purposeful; they just are.

The second characteristic of these laws is that they are presumed to be unchanging and without exception. In other words, these laws have not just existed since the beginning of the universe; they have always existed as the same laws, functioning with unwavering consistency. They dictate that a particular set of causal factors connected with a given set of conditions demand a specific effect, the exact same effect, whenever the same causes and conditions are in place. Therefore, if you drop a water balloon from the top of the Empire State Building (an activity strongly discouraged by the NYPD) with knowledge of all the relevant conditions and laws, you can predict exactly when and where it will land every time. As Malcolm Sayer put it, everything "has its place in that order. You can't change that." Order is provided by the unchangeable laws.

When the laws by which nature operates are described as uniform and without exception, this is not limited to nonhuman operations. Human beings are not a special case (so if you drop a human being from the top of the Empire State Building . . .). Since we are collections of matter that interact in lawful ways, our activities must be explored and explained in essentially the same manner we would investigate the lives of bovines or moss. Everything that happens to us or within us is subject to this intricate web of causal forces. Even our aspirations, emotions, thoughts, aesthetic judgments or moral choices are reducible to physical effects brought about by prior physical causes. Such human activities cannot be attributed to anything like a soul or mind since naturalism denies the existence of any nonphysical entity. All that we do must be traced to some physical organ such as a brain.

Another way of talking about the control of the laws of nature is to speak of determinism. If nonphysical things like souls or minds exist, we can conceive of how they would be exempt from causal laws that govern matter. Naturalism, however, discounts the existence of nonmaterial entities out of hand. Since everything is matter, and the laws of cause and effect apply in all cases, whatever occurs is determined. Things cannot be other than they are. Thus, the effects in a physical organ such as the brain are the inevitable result of previous causes. As a result, our entire story, like the story of the cosmos, is told most accurately in the language of chemistry, biology and physics, not the ideas of philosophy, religion or other nonscientific forms of explanation.

REASON AND NATURALISM

The consistency of nature's operations points toward another significant feature of naturalism. The fact that cause and effect can explain and predict so many things leads to the conclusion that the world is a reasonable place. If you heat water to 212 degrees Fahrenheit at sea level, it is reasonable to expect it to boil; if you reduce the temperature to 32 degrees, it is unreasonable to think that it will not freeze. The logical structure of the universe seems to dictate, then, that we should use our rational powers as navigational beacons within this universe. This explains why naturalism is not very tolerant of worldviews that make room for God or other forces beyond the nexus of cause and effect. Naturalists argue that exempting some parts of life from the process of cause and effect gets in the way of knowledge and progress. If the fundamental belief of naturalism is true (that all reality is physical and functions according to uniform laws), it is both irrational and futile to talk about God, miracles or souls. These things are illusions; and if they do not exist, they have no power to cause any type of effect. Therefore, if we want to bring about changes in the world and solve our problems, reliance on God stands in the way of real solutions.

To make their case, naturalists remind us of the radical changes that have occurred over the past generation because of scientific discovery or innovation. Life spans have increased dramatically because of medical breakthroughs. New hybrids developed in recent decades have produced amazing increases in crop yields, saving millions from starvation. Massive leaps forward have come in communications, transportation and economy because of the thoughtful application of scientific methods. Naturalists note that, until recently, little progress was made in dealing with premature death, starvation, poverty and the entire list of perennial problems. The difference, they would say, is that we have finally set science free from superstition.

Naturalism argues that scientific technology can solve even more problems if we rely on rationality. In short, naturalism views science as a form of salvation. If we are going to solve our problems, it must come through a rational understanding and use of the unchanging laws of nature to our benefit. Reliance on divine intervention or other non-physical sources for our salvation leads nowhere. We might just as well try to cure cancer by waving a bag of magic beans or predict hurricanes by using horoscopes written by divine monkeys. Naturalists argue that if we apply reason to what is real (matter) and true (the laws of cause and effect), we can solve our problems. When we move outside science, we hinder discovery and progress.

Naturalism as Religion

In 1933 a document titled *The Humanist Manifesto* was produced by a group of scholars. This *Manifesto* reflects the fundamental ideas of a naturalist worldview—affirmation of the world as self-existing rather than created, total identification of human beings with nature, the replacement of God with modern science, our need for reliance on reason rather than traditional religious ideas. The closing paragraph of *The Humanist Manifesto* contains two additional elements also characteristic of naturalism.

> So stand the theses of religious humanism. Though we consider the religious forms and ideas of our fathers no longer adequate, the quest for the good life is still the central task for mankind. Man is at last becoming aware that he alone is responsible for the realization of the world of his dreams, that he has within himself the power for its achievement. He must set intelligence and will to the task.

This concluding statement makes it clear that naturalism views itself as a religion, and one that stands in contrast to other religions. Like other religions, naturalism claims to provide a comprehensive worldview that applies to the whole of life and, as it is reflected here, offers a program to bridge differences between people. The second observation is closely related. Naturalism explicitly aims at the same goal other religions pursue—salvation. *The Humanist Manifesto* may speak of salvation in terms of "the good life" and "the world of [our] dreams," but the idea of attaining the most complete life possible, which is what salvation is about, is clearly there.

When naturalism starts with the premise that no divine reality or realities exist, we might assume that its goals are not as ambitious or all-encompassing as those offered by worldviews that include the divine. Such assumptions often cause us to minimize the importance of addressing naturalism as a direct competitor for the hearts and minds of people. However, we should take naturalism at its word. If it identifies itself as a religion, albeit a godless one, in competition with all other religions, naturalism's ambitions are far-reaching. In its claims to provide the best explanation of the world and its movements, the best and only means of achieving our broadest and highest aspirations in every aspect of life, and the best hope for overcoming the differences that separate people, naturalism has all the hallmarks of a religious system.

THE POSITIVE ASPECTS OF SCIENTIFIC NATURALISM

Many Christians correctly recognize that naturalism does not find belief in God as simply a benign belief but as a dangerous alternative to rational scientific techniques. As a result, Christians often incorrectly react by rejecting science itself (sometimes with a rejection of rationality thrown in for good measure) rather than naturalism. While naturalism as a comprehensive worldview is problematic, it includes elements such as science and reason that are themselves neither problematic nor worldviews. In fact, both should find prominent positions within any carefully crafted worldview, and to this extent, we need to understand what naturalism does right with its incorporation of these two elements.

1. Scientific naturalism recognizes the value of science. It is clear that certain types of questions are best answered by using scientific methods, and many of science's accomplishments have brought positive changes in our lives. Through the application of scientific principles to the world of medicine, for example, we have steadily increased life spans and cured previously incurable diseases. We have also seen the boundaries of other limitations pushed back by technology. Computers make calculations in a nanosecond that we could never make in a year without them. Technological advances have made travel faster, safer and more comfortable. We could multiply examples of useful contributions that have been generated by scientific explorations, many of which impact daily life at every turn.

Application of scientific methods to certain problems also bears out naturalism's claim that the laws of nature have a certain consistency and reliability. When the laws for a particular process are understood sufficiently and the conditions can be controlled, we are able to make predictions about outcomes. I have never really gotten over my juvenile fascination with explosions, so I was intrigued by a program about highly specialized teams that demolish huge structures. These experts use their knowledge of cause and effect to strategically place explosives and set them off in tightly choreographed sequences that cause a building or arena to collapse on itself, leaving other buildings just yards away rather dusty but otherwise undamaged. Such a feat is impossible unless we can count on the consistency of causation.

Our point here is rather simple, and we think it is also obvious. If we deny the validity and usefulness of the scientific method for controlling, creating and predicting certain products or events, we just end up looking silly. This does not mean that we have to concede the field to the naturalist worldview. Even if we agree (and we should) that scientific methods and knowledge supply a great deal of insight into ourselves and our universe, interesting debates still need to be engaged in about whether a scientific approach should be absolutized (as in naturalism) or whether it has limitations. These debates, some of which we will introduce later, are the real points of contention. However, when Christians offer wholesale dismissals of science or engage in knee-jerk reaction to new technological developments, we simply confirm one of the broadest caricatures that naturalists have about Christianity.

2. Scientific naturalism acknowledges the importance of reason. Naturalism, as we have seen, makes rationality the final arbiter of truth. In staking out this position, it often speaks of reason as the polar opposite of revelation, which is generally put into the category of superstition. The choice it poses, then, is an either-or decision—either reason or revelation. Some Christians have bought into that dualism by relying on revelation and exhibiting skepticism toward reason. However, the best Christian thinkers throughout history do not pit revelation and reason against each other (although deep disagreements exist concerning the proper relationship between reason and revelation).

At its most basic level, revelation requires rational capacities for understanding and interpretation. Thus, reason dictates that the statement "Jesus is Lord" means something very different from the proposition, "You, too, can talk in a Donald Duck voice if you stick bamboo in your ear." Even if "Jesus is Lord" is essentially a faith claim, the meaning involves interpretation, a process that involves our reason, to delineate what Jesus' lordship means and does not mean.

Another way to frame this point is to recognize naturalism's concern to determine what is factual about the universe. Because naturalism believes that reliance on fictions, falsehoods and illusions holds us back from the truths that can set us free, it is very rigorous in its quest for facts. Christians ought to applaud this goal enthusiastically. Here's the rub, though. Just as naturalism sets reason and revelation in opposition, it also views the realm of fact as one that excludes faith. In other words, it sets up a fact-faith dualism; you can either rely on fact or faith, but you cannot do both.

We believe that this is a false dilemma. Some faith claims are also factual, even if not verifiable by the same means as scientific facts such as the circumference of the moon. Moreover, we will argue later that naturalism is as much of a faith position as Christianity is. If this is correct, the real tension between Christianity and naturalism is not whether one should rely only on reason or revelation, or whether our dependence should be placed in fact or faith. Instead, the question is which faith system, naturalism or Christianity, provides the more factual picture of the universe and is therefore the more reasonable worldview to invest our lives in.

3. Scientific naturalism is correct in its quest for unity and its desire to solve earthly problems. One final positive aspect of humanistic naturalism is its recognition that the human race is often divided when it should be unified. Our divisions are not simply neutral facts about human history, but bear within them the destructive elements of war, colonization, slavery, impoverishment and deprivation of basic human rights. Naturalism has a strong commitment to the commonality of human nature. People everywhere are made of the same stuff and are subject to the same laws of nature. More importantly, they all share the same rationality. It follows, therefore, that the shared elements of human existence should be of more significance than secondary matters such as race, language, geographic location and other things that distinguish us from each other. If we recognize our common humanity, naturalism claims, we can get down to the business of finding answers for entrenched problems that diminish both the quantity and quality of our existence.

This also helps us understand naturalism's active opposition to religion. As painful as it is for people of faith to admit, religion often has been used as justification for many of the most divisive and devastating struggles in history. In the light of this history, naturalism strongly doubts that religion will ever bring unity to all people. It concludes, therefore, that if humanity is to find common ground and healing for the struggles that have plagued us, traditional religion must be replaced by a rational worldview.

Naturalism's dream of unifying the human race on the basis of a rationality that transcends all culture assumes that reason is neutral and objective. This assumption encounters difficulty if the concept of an unbiased rationality is an outmoded remnant of the Enlightenment. In fact, doubts about the objectivity of reason have dealt severe blows to naturalism in recent years (see chapter eight). However, even if reason can stand untarnished by cultural and historical influences, we still have to assume that this transcendent reason will exert such control over our moral will that, under its sway, we will act in benevolent ways toward all, regardless of who or where they are. Science provides tools for explaining what we *can* do, but by itself it does not offer much direction about what we *should* do.

Moreover, while naturalism is quick to promote all the good that has come about from technology, it seldom reminds us that the same technologies that may increase energy supplies or cure diseases also can be used to quickly kill billions. Unfortunately, naturalism provides little assurance that those with the power to control the forces of the universe will use those powers for good, and history does not bear out the premise that advances in knowledge correspond to similar advances in compassion, justice and kindness.

Despite its rather unrealistic faith that reason will make us a more moral or unified race, naturalism understands clearly that the horrific consequences of our disunity stand as a tragic testimony that something has gone wrong and that this history is condemned to simply repeat itself unless we find a common ground. In this way, naturalism reminds Christians of two related elements that should be incorporated into a comprehensive worldview. First, our worldview must offer a reality that transcends culture and provides a solid foundation for a unified humanity. Second, naturalism reminds us that working to overcome our legacy of destructive divisiveness should not be postponed to the hereafter. This task must be engaged fully in the here and now.

POTENTIAL PROBLEMS IN NATURALISM

We have already mentioned that scientific naturalism should be viewed as a form of religion, and it describes itself as such in *The Humanist Manifesto*. In 1973, *The Humanist Manifesto II*, an updated version of the original *Manifesto*, appeared (although it tones down the idea that it is a form of religion). Its introductory section provides a nice summary of naturalism's concept of salvation and the means for achieving it:

> The next century can be and should be the humanistic century. Dramatic scientific, technological, and ever-accelerating social and political changes crowd our awareness. We have virtually conquered the planet, explored the moon, overcome the natural limits of travel and communication; we stand at the dawn of a new age, ready to move farther into space and perhaps inhabit other planets. Using technology wisely, we can control our environment, conquer poverty, markedly reduce disease, extend our life-span, significantly modify our behavior, alter the course

of human evolution and cultural development, unlock vast new powers, and provide humankind with unparalleled opportunity for achieving an abundant and meaningful life.[1]

This list of "salvation goals" reflects naturalism's materialistic foundation by limiting its aims to this world and this life. This makes sense within naturalism's metaphysics. When my biological functions cease, *I* cease to exist. The matter of which I am made continues, but *I* don't exist eternally. Moreover, in naturalism's closed system, there is no place for me to exist other than this universe. Therefore, *my* salvation has to be defined as a quantitative increase in my biological life span and a better quality of existence. Thus, while naturalism presents itself as an agenda for salvation, it is also conscious that its scope of salvation is modest in comparison to alternative salvation plans.

The second observation follows closely. The only resources by which we can accomplish the goals listed above must come from our own efforts. The system is closed and nothing exists outside of it. We cannot call for reinforcements. At the same time, *The Humanist Manifesto II* is very optimistic that we don't need reinforcements. These aims are achievable if we harness the powers of science and technology. We may have failed miserably in the past, but naturalism argues that our future is bright if we allow scientific rationality to show us the way.

While naturalism is consistent with its materialistic metaphysics in defining the scope of salvation and the tools available to accomplish this task, we will argue that this same metaphysical model creates two major obstacles. The first hurdle is that naturalism's concept of reality, and thus its plan of salvation, is too modest to encompass every aspect of human experience. If important parts of reality are left out of this worldview's metaphysics, and we think they are, these parts will also be left outside the scope of repair and redemption. The second obstacle is that naturalism's worldview provides insufficient tools to either justify or successfully accomplish its already modest salvation plan. In short,

---

[1]For the text of the original *Humanist Manifesto* and the two more recent versions of it, see the American Humanist website <www.americanhumanist.org>.

we will argue reality is bigger than naturalism recognizes and that its resources are smaller and less potent than it assumes.

1. Scientific naturalism diminishes the status of human beings. Naturalism really began to gain its foothold around the eighteenth century, about the same time scientists started to grasp the utter vastness of our cosmos. The parallel development of these two factors seems ironic. If human beings consist of nothing more than a miniscule fraction of nature's stuff, and if we realize how much stuff is contained in our almost unthinkably huge universe, the logical conclusion would seem to be that we humans are infinitesimally dinky nothings located at an insignificant place in an impersonal universe. But this is not the conclusion naturalism has drawn. It considers us the center of this universe, with the power to control our environment through technology. If naturalism's metaphysics levels off existence, reducing everything to matter, the immensity of the cosmos also seems to radically relativize our significance.

Even when we focus on human life on this planet, it is hard to see how naturalism can explain the unique place and role it assigns to human beings. In the section cited above from *The Humanist Manifesto II*, it is clear that humanity is viewed as a special species. Humans alone "have virtually conquered the planet . . . [and] can control our environment, conquer poverty, and provide humankind with unparalleled opportunity for achieving an abundant and meaningful life." Nowhere does *Manifesto II* imply that kangaroos, poison ivy and the backyard fence can pull off these tasks. What makes us so special?

Naturalism is not alone in singling out the human race as uniquely endowed with distinctive powers and possibilities. Throughout our intellectual history, human beings were thought to occupy a unique location in the universe. While aware that humans are closely connected with the nonhuman realm, the vast majority also argued that human beings possess a special "something" that sets us apart. The specific nature of that special "something" has generated considerable debate, but most of the answers revolved around a divine Being or beings and the soul, and usually these elements were combined.

Those who spoke of human uniqueness and superiority to the nonhuman domain readily admitted their inability to observe God or the soul directly, but they found such realities to be justified because of what they could observe. Simply put, human beings engage in a broad variety of activities not found in other species. Humans create art, fall in love, make moral evaluations, form communities based on interests and religion, think about the meaning of life, invent worldviews and write books about all these things. Since animals have the same fundamental material composition and organs that perform the same operations as in humans, it seemed sensible to them, to believe that uniquely human functions originated from some other source than the body.

This little bit of history is important because naturalism, as we have seen, wants us to get rid of God or the soul. Everything—human beings, kangaroos, poison ivy and the backyard fence—consists of the same basic matter, and nothing else. Thus, when the materialist Ludwig Feuerbach said "You are what you eat," he was offering a metaphysical statement rather than a commentary on dietary practices. He meant that the basic components of lunch are the same types of things of which you consist. Reality is reducible to matter and its activities. No room exists in this metaphysical paradigm for God or a soul. At the same time, however, naturalists reserve a special place in the universe for human beings.

The issue is not whether human beings should continue to make aesthetic evaluations, moral choices, perform operas and cancer surgery, or fall in love and get married. Perhaps with the exception of opera, almost everyone agrees that we can or should engage in these purely human activities. The question is whether naturalism can explain *how* we do these unique things if there is nothing unique about the human beings who do these things. This is a general statement of a problem that we will break down into specific questions in the following criticisms.

2. Can matter be moral? If we glance back over the goals in *Manifesto II*, we will recognize that they are *moral* goals. Even though they don't use the word there, the framers of *The Humanist Manifesto II* were clearly talking about ethics since they proposed that we *should* do certain things and stop doing others. However, because of the assertion that human beings are comprised of matter alone, we are immediately confronted with a question: Can merely material beings have moral characteristics?

I can't say that I'm aware of anyone willing to claim moral attributes for raw matter. But if a single atom is not a moral entity, how is it possible for any collection of amoral atoms to be or become a moral entity, even if that collection of atoms happens to be a human being? How do beings consisting of nonmoral matter aspire to moral goals?

Naturalism seems to dig its hole even deeper when it claims that change in matter is generated by the laws of nature. Even if (here we have a huge if) a particular conglomeration of matter can be moral, we also have to assume that the principles that generate change in matter also have a moral character. Again, however, naturalism makes no such claim for the laws of nature. Instead, the driving forces behind nature are viewed as impersonal. The laws of nature may tell us why something *is* the way it is or why something *will be* in a certain state given the proper conditions, but this is different from explaining how things *should* be. And moral claims are statements about how things *should* be.

This brings us back to the question of determinism. Most naturalists believe that cause and effect encompasses everything and that events cannot be other than they are. At the same time, they assume that we have a responsibility for what happens in and to the universe. Our intuition seems to say that these two views are incompatible; to the extent that things are outside our control, we cannot be held responsible. To be fair, some scholars hold a position known as *compatibilism*, which argues that determinism, whether caused by a sovereign God or a sovereign set of natural laws, is compatible with human responsibility. Although we do not have the space to examine these highly complex theories, let me offer my own quick evaluation. When determinism results from a sovereign God who is inherently moral, this leaves room to talk about our own moral responsibility (although we think that defining sovereignty in a way that does not entail determinism is a more promising solution). However, if the laws of nature are both inherently amoral *and* completely deterministic, it is hard to see where moral responsibility finds a home in scientific naturalism's universe.

Here's a slightly different way of stating the situation above. Both theists and naturalists share the belief that we have ethical responsibilities and should strive for the good. For the theist, the idea of a moral God helps explain our own moral impulse. The intellectual problem faced by theists, then, is why so much evil exists in a world created by a good God—the so-called problem of evil. Anyone who has tried to work this out will acknowledge the difficulties, although the concept of a moral and volitional God who creates human beings in his image offers something to work with. For naturalists, the problem is different. They have what one might call a "problem of good" because they have to explain the origin of good (and evil, for that matter) in a world consisting of amoral matter whose course is unswervingly determined by impersonal forces. If the cosmos is closed and its fundamental principles are not inherently moral, how does the idea of moral good even arise?

3. Scientific naturalism undercuts rationality. Naturalism argues that reason, or more specifically, scientific rationality, is the means by which we can bring an end to human suffering and deprivation. However, the paradigm by which naturalism operates calls into question the status of reason itself. The problem is very cogently summarized by C. S. Lewis's response to the idea that our solar system and life in the universe was brought about by an accidental ("accidental" here refers to events that are not willed or chosen but are the result of laws operating on material forces) stellar collision. Lewis says,

> If the solar system was brought about by an accidental collision, then the appearance of organic life on this planet was also an accident, and the whole evolution of Man was an accident too. If so, then all our present thoughts are mere accidents—the accidental by-product of the movement of atoms. And this holds for the thoughts of the materialists and astronomers as well as for anyone else's. But if *their* thoughts—i.e., of Materialism and Astronomy—are merely accidental by-products, why should we believe them to be true? I see no reason for believing that one accident should be able to give me a correct account of all the other accidents. It's like expecting that the accidental shape taken by the splash when you upset a milk-jug should give you a correct account of how the jug was made and why it was upset.[2]

---

[2]C. S. Lewis, *God in the Dock: Essays on Theology and Ethics* (Grand Rapids: Eerdmans, 1970), pp. 52-53.

In this selection, Lewis points out something easy to forget. If reason is to bring about the betterment of humanity, it must stand outside the processes it hopes to change. However, for naturalism, our reason is not simply involved in the progression of material forces; it is the *result* of them. Our thoughts are completely dependent on the same causal factors that determine the universe we seek to control.

4. Scientific naturalism cannot define progress or explain purpose. Naturalism speaks of the laws of nature as the force that gives direction to the process of change. However, we need to be careful what we mean when we speak of direction. "Direction" *can* imply that some goal or purpose exists for a process of change. So when we stop to get directions to some location (unlikely if a guy is driving), our destination is the goal. Under a naturalistic worldview, however, it is difficult to speak of unintentional and impersonal processes of change as possessing purpose or to regard them as progress. Yet, naturalism sells itself as the means of progress and moral advance.

The reasons why a naturalistic worldview does not accommodate the ideas of progress and purpose can be masked by our references to the governing forces behind change as *laws*. Language about laws refers to what *should* or *should not* be done. If there is a moral law about respecting human life, it tells us how we *should* treat people. Traffic laws inform us that we *should not* drive faster than the posted speed limits. In both cases, we have a choice about whether we will obey these laws. Choice does not come into play, however, when we speak of the laws of nature. Nature's laws do not flex for exceptions. They tell us what *is* going to happen under a certain set of circumstances. But there's no choosing here.

The difference between these two types of laws is that laws of nature are *descriptive*. They describe how things are or how things will be under particular conditions. In contrast, moral, civil or criminal types of laws are *prescriptive*. They tell us what we should do. Here's the rub. When we say that things or people have a purpose, this prescribes how something *should* be. In such prescriptions, our purpose will not be achieved if the wrong choices are made. However, if everything falls under the domain of nature's laws, as naturalism proposes, things cannot be other than what they are.

Naturalism encounters another problem when it comes to the idea of progress, since a system of eternal change does not appear to offer any idea of what we should progress *toward*. Things may be changing, but to know whether change is good or bad movement, we have to have some idea of the *telos* or goal. Naturalism clearly believes that eliminating disease, war and poverty constitutes progress. However, naturalism cannot tell us *why* health is better than disease or peace is preferable to war. Every state is simply a specific configuration of atoms. The laws of nature may describe which configuration of atoms in an organism is a healthy one, but that is very different from explaining why one configuration of atoms is better than another.

It is also unclear why naturalism defines progress by reference to human beings rather than some other form of existence, living or not. If both human beings and bacteria consist of essentially the same matter and are subject to the same set of laws, why should human flourishing be favored over the healthy multiplication of a bacterial colony? Human life may be more complex than bacterial life, but complexity in itself does not mean that it is better or more valuable. In short, the basic assumptions of naturalism make it difficult to see how any talk about values, purposes or progress can be wedged into this worldview.

CONCLUSION

An anecdote that has made its way through Christian circles provides a good point of departure to summarize the shortcomings of naturalism. It tells of a group of scientists who go to God, asserting that he is no longer necessary since they have harnessed the powers of science sufficiently to create human life. Intrigued by this, God asks for a demonstration. One scientist reaches down and grabs a handful of dirt to begin the process. At this point, God stops him and says, "Get your own dirt."

This little story highlights a critical distinction that we often fail to make—the distinction between fabrication and creation. Fabrication, taking raw materials and reshaping them into different forms, is a realm where some amazing things have been accomplished by means of scientific methods. It is conceivable that somewhere in the future, human life will be fabricated out of the components present in dirt. After all, that is essentially what we return to after we check out biologically. Such a technological feat would involve significant quantities of knowledge, but the knowledge required to fabricate a human being from dust still leaves a basic question unanswered. It doesn't tell us how the dirt came to be there in the first place, how it was created. In fact, naturalism sidesteps the question of the dirt's ultimate origin completely by claiming that matter exists eternally.

Christianity holds an alternative view to naturalism's idea that matter, or whatever stands behind matter, is eternal. It speaks, not of fabrication only, but also of *creation*, a process by which God brought dirt and other forms of matter into being out of nothing. This is admittedly a faith position. I doubt that the statement "God created the multiple somethings of the universe out of an empty nothing" can be proved, and I know it can't be demonstrated to be a factual statement by naturalism's criteria. However, naturalism also cannot demonstrate that "matter exists eternally" is a factual statement by its own criteria. Naturalism's ideas of the nature of matter, the uniformity of nature's laws and the sovereignty of reason may allow us to *claim* that matter is eternal, but no combination of these concepts supplies proof that this assertion is a fact. The statement "matter is eternal" is no less a faith claim than "God created matter."

Our conclusion that naturalism is a faith system is not simply built on its premise that matter is eternal, but is another way of restating the critiques above. When we argue that naturalism's assertions about morality, human uniqueness and superiority, rationality and purpose cannot be justified as factual statements by the very standards it has established, we are saying that each of these positions requires a significant element of faith. Moreover, we would say that these are misdirected faith statements.

What separates a good faith statement from one that should be discarded is a complicated matter, but at least one measure should be internal consistency, and naturalism fails on this count. Its worldview starts from the premises that everything is comprised of eternally existing matter operating under unchangeable laws of nature. Everything is contained in a system that is locked down; nothing enters or leaves.

These are statements of faith and, as they stand here, they have a sig-nificant degree of logical consistency. The problem comes when we try to explain how even the most basic elements of human experience fit into this system. How can we expect collections of amoral atoms to as-sume moral responsibility? Does it make any sense to think of love ra-diating out of clumps of protons and electrons? Can clusters of carbon think? Why do neurons react in ways that cause human beings, and only human beings, to wonder why we exist in the first place and what our purpose should be during the course of our existence?

The inconsistency in naturalism's faith system arises because it starts with a closed system comprised of impersonal matter ruled by imper-sonal laws, but seeks to maintain all the elements of personal and meaningful life. It has been observed that the beliefs of many natural-ists basically amount to Christianity minus God. All the ethics, poten-tial, significance and glory are the same as those found in Christianity, but without God as the foundation. In short, naturalism smuggles all the features of personal and goal-directed existence through an open back door of an impersonal universe that is supposed to be closed. It is a bit like trying to add up a bunch of finite numbers to arrive at an in-finite number.

Christianity begins with faith claims that include a God who is per-sonal by nature and creates a universe open to his influence. The uni-verse's openness to a personal God gives us a toehold for speaking about morality, beauty, value, purpose and all the other things that need to be incorporated if we are going to describe the world consistently. When you start from a rational Creator, you have the raw materials to explain why nature is governed by rational and consistent laws. Christianity is, to be sure, a faith system. I can't explain how God happens to be eternal or how he creates something from nothing. It takes some faith to be-lieve these things, but not near as much faith as it takes to believe that love is possible in a world that is essentially impersonal.

Many find naturalism attractive because it seems to be a more mod-ern worldview that offers objectivity and certainty. However, world-views that attempt to reduce reality to matter have been around since the beginning of Western philosophy, and have always been minority positions for essentially the same reasons we noted above. It just does not seem possible to explain why human beings do what they do in a closed material universe. In more recent years, additional objections, which we have mentioned briefly above, have been raised. First, many question whether the level of rational objectivity and intellectual neutrality assumed in naturalism is possible. Since we are so strongly influenced by historical and cultural factors, the belief that we can or will view the universe as unbiased observers and moral agents is certainly open to criticism. While, as noted above, contemporary naturalism promotes the unity of humanity, the social evolutionary naturalism of the nineteenth century often used the same premises to support the separation of the races. Though it would like to argue that it is not the case, science cannot be easily separated from the reigning ideologies of the age. Second, the uniformity of natural laws assumed in naturalism has come under severe criticism from science itself, particularly physics, which argues that a considerable element of uncertainty and randomness is built into the processes of change.

The criticism of naturalism from science itself provides a good reminder that, even though naturalism finds scientific reasoning as the foundation for its worldview, this does not mean that science itself implies naturalism or that all scientists adopt a naturalistic worldview. In fact, I would venture to guess that scientists who reflect carefully on their fields are less likely to be naturalists than nonscientists, because they clearly recognize the limitations inherent in the sciences. Those who adopt naturalism are attracted by the features we note above—the promise of controlling the powers of the cosmos with tools that are objective, certain and fully rational. Our examination concludes that naturalism cannot deliver on this promise.

THE NEW AGE

Are We Gods or Are We God's?

IF YOU BEGIN WITH A LARGE PORTION of American individualism, throw in a generous dose of Eastern mysticism, and add a pinch of rebellion against consumerism, tradition and Enlightenment rationalism, what do you get? What we have above are some of the main ingredients for a wide-ranging, amorphous movement commonly called New Age.

The New Age label has been attached to areas as diverse as education, politics, religion, health (including dentistry), music, business and psychology, yet you will rarely find people who identify themselves as New Agers in the way that someone might identify themselves as Protestant, Democrat or a soccer player. It encompasses such varied practices as yoga, shamanism, hypnosis, past-life regression, crystal and pyramid healing, and chromotherapy, just to name a few, so it defies definition by any creed or set of doctrines. While you could find a multitude of businesses, seminars, publishers, communes and institutes given to various New Age ideas and practices, the movement has no organizational or institutional center. Given this, one would not go too far afield in suspecting that any attempt to define New Age is like trying to nail Jell-O to a wall. In some ways, the New Age is like the Internet; it is both nowhere and everywhere. While the New Age movement is tricky to pin down with precision, it is out there. We can get a working description by examining its goals, what it defines itself against, the sources it draws from and its fundamental characteristics.

Perhaps a good general description of the New Age movement's aim is that it endeavors to help individuals recognize their inner divinity, which goes by a number of names, such as God-consciousness or Higher Self. Whatever we call it, once we become conscious of this interior force, we can actualize this vast reservoir of dormant potential within us. Implicit in this idea is that our capacities extend well beyond the range of our present abilities. The problem is ignorance. We are unaware of these untapped powers, and this lack of consciousness places unnecessary limits on us and keeps us from breaking free of old patterns and boundaries.

Thus, the "New" in New Age signals this movement's dissatisfaction with both present and past. This broad coalition tends to view the universe as an evolving entity, and says that this evolution requires transcendence of the present mindsets that create mental hindrances and keep us from full realization of our own potential. The New Age identifies a number of culprits that keep us trapped. It wants to get beyond the old assumptions of naturalism, which reject the spiritual dimension of life. It registers discontent with the past's faith that technology will resolve all our problems. New Agers believe that organized religion has been too exclusive, and that media, politics and culture in general have lost their souls. In short, the New Age believes that the "old age" uses definitions of reason and truth that squeeze us into self-imposed mental prisons, restricting our freedom and our vast possibilities. The old age has failed; we need a New Age.

The vision of the coming New Age is about as varied as the movement itself. Sometimes it is portrayed in rather modest terms of personal spiritual enlightenment and peace. Usually, however, this personal spiritual attunement is viewed as a harbinger of a universal New Age. Many advocates anticipate that the convergence of individuals realizing their divinity will bring about a profound change in which long-standing barriers created by race, nationality, religion and other factors fade into the past. We will experience freedom from disease, peaceful coexistence with our environment, the elimination of poverty and warfare, and perhaps even a Chicago Cubs World Series victory. In short, many New Agers view the emerging era, not just in terms of individual salvation, but as a universal salvation.

WEST MEETS EAST

As an alternative to the stifling effect of the "old age's" limitations, the New Age draws from two main streams that represent a unique fusion of East and West. As we will see below, the Western stream contributes the individualistic tendencies found in New Age. The eastern tributary, which we will begin with, provides the monistic foundation for the movement. *Monism,* in general, refers to the unity of all things. The New Age's monism stands in contrast to common Western dualisms that distinguish between body and soul, God and nature, reason and imagination, time and eternity, even right and wrong. As we will see below, New Age thinkers find these dualisms at the root of our most fundamental problems. For now, it is important to recognize that the New Age sees these dualisms as illusion. Reality constitutes an indivisible whole, a unity that does not allow for the strong distinctions between things generally assumed in "old age" Western philosophies.

In place of the dualism that sets God as distinct from nature, New Age offers two closely related forms of monism. One version, pantheism, says that everything that exists is divine. There is no part of nature that is not God; no part of the divine is outside the universe. God equals the universe in its totality. The second version, pan*en*theism, agrees that all of nature is divine, but also says that an aspect of the divine exists beyond the universe. New Agers differ on the question of whether God is identical with the universe or transcends it in some way, but they are united in what pantheism and panentheism agree on: everything is infused with the divine. Of course, this "everything" includes us. Whether we know it or not, the divine powers of the cosmos are not just available to us; they *are* us. And unleashing these spiritual energies is the path to both personal and universal enlightenment and betterment. Thus, the New Age movement promises the keys by which we can unlock our inner, unused divine power.

At this point, Eastern monism is fused with Western individualism. For the New Age, there is no single "right way" to gain access to the divine within. Our full potential is achieved by means as varied as the personalities of the seekers. On a recent afternoon at a coffee shop, I picked up a New Age newspaper. Inside, I found such diverse offerings as Zen workshops, past-life regression therapy, goddess worship, spiritual guides, tarot reading, biofeedback, herbal medicines, Wiccan practitioners, channeling, Reiki, yoga, ecofeminism, and the catalog goes on from there.

Because of this broad diversity in practices, New Age is often referred to as a syncretistic approach to salvation. However, this might imply that the various practices and ideas could in some way be synchronized into a coherent whole. This is not the case. Instead, *eclecticism* gives a more accurate description of New Age's individualistic tone. If the advocates of each specific methodology noted in the newspaper above believe their practice or belief is the only true way, it was never evident. Instead, the clear message seems to be that New Age consumers should mix and match until they find the formula that is right for them. The paths to enlightenment are many, and each person is encouraged to explore different options until they find their own route. This strong individualistic tendency, by the way, means that many of the criticisms we make concerning individualism itself in chapter two are valid for the New Age movement as well, even though we will not repeat them in our evaluation section for this chapter.

Unleashing Our Higher Self

From what we have seen above, it is evident that New Age makes some very big claims. It envisions a radically new world in the future, not just a series of incremental improvements. Followers claim much more than the possibility of drawing on God's power or a relationship with the divine. Instead, they say that we *are* gods. The natural question from those skeptical of New Age thought, then, is why we have so many limitations on our spiritual energies if each person embodies the divine.

If all the ingredients for this amazing New Age are already within us, why has it not come about before this? Advocates of New Age might respond that we cannot draw on the spiritual power within if we do not realize it is there, and this lack of awareness results from dualism.

Dualism has a long history in Western intellectual and religious traditions. One of its most famous advocates is Plato, who drew a heavy distinction between the physical and nonphysical worlds. He included divine realities and our souls in the nonphysical realm, and elevated this to a superior position over the changeable, physical realm. Moreover, the divine and intangible took priority because he thought they were known by reason, while physical objects underwent change and were known by our imperfect senses. As time went on, important strands of Western thought maintained Plato's emphasis on rationality as our access to truth, but little by little, moved to a more empirical model that placed the emphasis on the physical world. In many cases, this emphasis was so strong that the nonphysical realm was defined right out of existence (as in scientific naturalism). In other cases, the dualism of body and soul or God and nature remained, but Plato's priority of the nonphysical over the physical realm was inverted, as we will see below. Christian thought also maintained a distinction between the nonphysical and the physical in ways that roughly parallel Plato's version, but with an important variation. In the Christian story, nature is a creation of God. However, the created realm, which includes human beings, has fallen from its original state of purity and requires a Savior to restore it.

This rather long excursus on dualism brings us back to the New Ager's position. It says that the modern mind, under the influence of dualistic thought, either rejects the existence of a spiritual dimension (materialism) or assumes that created reality is separate and estranged from God. As a result, we never entertain the possibility that the divine, and our salvation, is within us. We have wasted history by looking for salvation in all the wrong places. The New Age movement says that our first step is to throw off these materialistic or dualistic ideas and recognize that the divine is not some distant, transcendent entity who remains outside us. Instead, the spiritual force is within us, and within all of nature for that matter. Likewise, if we see nature as an interconnected spiritual reality, God will be evident in all things because God *is* all things. Thus, when we know *where* to look for the divine, we have taken the first step toward discovering the Higher Self buried within. The next step is discovering *how* to uncover and release the energies of this Higher Self.

GNOSIS VERSUS LOGOS

A second move that occurred during the Enlightenment is that Plato's dualism was turned on its head. Rather than relegating empirical realities such as birds, dirt, steel beams and human bodies to a place of secondary importance, as Plato did, they are now the things we know by reason. For many in the Enlightenment, physical objects became the only realities about which we could have certain, objective knowledge. In contrast, nontangible realities such as goodness, God or the soul were thought to stand outside the boundaries of rationality. Thus, they were placed in the category of the subjective. These things might have personal significance, but our ideas about them are not "real" knowledge because there is no way to empirically verify our claims about them. In this case, the dualism remains, but spiritual truth is denigrated as mere intuition, personal preference or individual experience.

New Agers argue that when we limit the realm of truth to the material realm, we cease to comprehend the spiritual dimension. Therefore, to see beyond the merely external aspects of nature, we need a new type of knowledge. Instead of relying on *logos,* the left-brain, linear form of logic favored by the Enlightenment, the New Age movement seeks *gnosis. Gnosis* comes from a Greek term that refers to forms of knowledge that are mystical and intuitive. Instead of restricting knowledge to the left side of the brain, which processes information gathered via the senses, we need to nurture the creative and intuitive capacities of our brain's right hemisphere. This is the home of our Higher Self, the world that reaches beyond the mere causes and effects of material objects.

Logos reasoning looks at the world in a mechanistic way. Every observable effect, if it is to be understood and properly modified, must be traced back to a similarly measurable cause. This type of rationality works well for identifying what type of bacteria causes a particular type of infection, and it comes in really handy if you are trying to repair a diesel engine. But if the world if not just a machine, if our "Higher Self" is beyond cause and effect, mechanical knowledge is insufficient for curing whatever ails our inner spirit. Thus, New Age publications tout the powers of neopagan rituals, aura reading (and even aura massage), chanting, crystals and scores of other practices to awaken our latent gnosis and actualize the vast resources of our Higher Being.

Of course, such methods will strike outsiders as a bit loony, to put it bluntly. Tarot cards, ESP and channeling the spirits of the dead all stand well outside the chain of cause and effect, and there is no way to empirically test whether such methods actually evoke our Higher Self. For that matter, we cannot even empirically demonstrate that anything like a Higher Self exists in order to be stirred by such means.

At this point, a New Age response might go something like this. If your form of logos, your rationality, reduces the world to a complex, physical mechanism, you forfeit any real meaning, purpose or spirituality in the world. Yet the vast majority of human beings that have ever inhabited this world cannot seem to help but believe that they can make contact with the divine force. Moreover, their experience with this spiritual reality is the foundation on which they find meaning. Thus, the New Ager might continue, isn't it a bit arbitrary to elevate the materialistic realm to the level of highest importance? Isn't it arrogant to limit words like *truth* and *knowledge* to the world of observable and measurable objects and overlook the subjective realm, which is the very source of our sense of goodness, purpose and spirituality?

The New Age thus argues that we should return the spiritual sphere to the place of first importance that it has occupied throughout human history. As a parallel move, gnosis is likewise given prominence while logos is thus demoted to a secondary role. In many cases within New Age monism, the very existence of the physical realm as something distinct from the cosmic divine is viewed as an illusion that must be overcome. An example of this view is found in a scene from the *Matrix*, where a young boy is bending a spoon. Neo picks up a spoon and attempts to bend it, unsuccessfully. The boy tells Neo, "Your spoon does not bend because it is just that, a spoon. Mine bends because there is no spoon, just my mind," as his spoon is twisted into a knot. The boy continues, "Link yourself to the spoon. Become the spoon and bend yourself." As Neo focuses on the spoon, it begins to bend.

At this juncture, we might grasp these key characteristics of New Age by comparing two interesting points of divergence with scientific naturalism. First, both New Age and naturalism are monistic, but they disagree about the nature of this single reality. Scientific naturalism reduces everything to matter. Mind, soul and God are illusions. In contrast, the New Age worldview relegates the physical to the category of nonexistence or absorbs it into a divine force that is the only true reality.

Second, both New Age and scientific naturalism view ignorance as our fundamental barrier to truth and salvation; both seek enlightenment. The important difference here, however, is that logos of the historical Enlightenment is the key to our freedom within the naturalist's worldview. Rationality saves us from the superstitions of the past's supernaturalism. The New Ager envisions a totally different type of enlightenment, however. Gnosis frees us from the shackles of dualism and allows us to see the universe for what it really is—a unified spiritual entity.

If New Age approaches to enlightenment are not subject to the type of testing and observation that might by applied to physical interactions, then how does one verify the validity of New Age claims and practices? The answer, in a nutshell, is that the proof is experiential. When something awakens our divine consciousness, we know it inwardly. Thus, the eclecticism and individualism reflected in the wide range of New Age practices corresponds to an eclectic and individualistic approach to verification. No one can prove or disprove the rightness of any New Age practice for another person because no one lives the experience of another person. If the physical world is, at most, a dim reflection of the real divine world, nothing in the external aspects of my life provides foolproof evidence of spiritual stirrings. The strongest evidence of activity within the Higher Self will be internal, subjective experiences. Given the private nature of such experience, then, methods that awaken my god-consciousness may differ from those that enliven you.

THE QUEST FOR HOLISM AND UNITY

New Age monism says that what we commonly experience as diversity is only a temporary or illusory manifestation of a single divine mind. This leads to an emphasis on holism and collectivism. If we recognize that body and soul are one or that we are not ultimately distinct from God, a tree or a computer, we can begin to understand political, economic, ethical and religious commitments frequently found in this coalition. Worldviews and political positions that emphasize linguistic, racial or national difference or uniqueness (such as postmodern tribalism [chapter eight] and nationalism [chapter four]) will be viewed as misguided. Instead, New Age politics seeks to remove national, ethnic, religious and racial boundaries in favor of "one world" politics. If my existence and well-being cannot be isolated from other human beings, resolving economic disparities between people becomes a moral mandate. Environmentalism is a common form of activism within the New Age coalition as a goal of holistic existence. Religious exclusivism has been a major source of strife between people throughout history. Thus, New Agers often seek to bring all spiritual quests under a single umbrella that more closely corresponds to the unity of reality. Not surprisingly, since the New Age believes that it makes no such exclusivist claims, it argues that all religions should be absorbed into it.

While New Age proponents are quite willing to take firm moral positions on corporate ethics, they are notoriously opposed to any sorts of restrictions on individual behaviors. Quite often this is hitched to the combination of monism and individualism within the movement. If we are each and all gods, then the only thing that counts as sin are actions we deem harmful to us or our god-consciousness. Thus, New Agers are commonly opposed to any laws or moral limitations on moral issues such as drug use, abortion, marital fidelity, suicide and similar issues. One oddity of New Age, then, is the coexistence of an almost fundamentalist approach to collective ethics with a laissez-faire attitude toward individual morality.

CHRISTIANS AND NEW AGE

Before we begin a focused evaluation of New Age, we want to make some preliminary comments about a Christian response to this worldview. On the one hand, Christians often overstate the threat of New Age. It is certainly not, as we have heard it portrayed in some Christian circles, a conspiracy bent on taking over the world. The strong individualism and eclecticism of the New Age work against almost any form of organization. For all of its emphasis on holism and unity, New Agers generally expend a good deal more energy arguing with each other than hatching global takeover plans. Moreover, the number of people who fit the composite description outlined above is comparatively small. Instead, most people absorb bits and pieces of New Age thought from cultural trends with little awareness of the core beliefs held by "true believers."

On the other hand, the fact that New Age ideas are so pervasive in culture is precisely what makes it a threat, and Christians are not immune from this influence. It may be impossible to discern whether it comes directly from the New Age movement or simply as a reaction (or overreaction) to the same things New Agers oppose, but many Christians clearly appropriate New Age–type ideas. For example, some Christians look at Scripture as the vessel of esoteric knowledge that liberates us from the mundane. Recent fascination with the so-called Bible code, which finds hidden messages from God that offer gnostic insight leading to salvation, parallels a New Age quest for such knowledge. In a similar way, many interpret Christian symbols or practices as having some sort of magical power. This magical view implies that we can harness God's power for our purposes if we just discover the right triggers and tease out hidden knowledge rather than viewing them as ways in which we submit our will to God's. Another New Age similarity would be attributing shamanistic or magical powers to those who supposedly have special access to divine knowledge or power.

Perhaps the three most prevalent New Age influences (or, at least, parallels) on contemporary Christianity are its individualism/subjectivism, anti-intellectualism and its denigration of the physical realm. Christians often form beliefs or base actions on private experiences or interpretations. When these are not subjected to scrutiny by Scripture, reason or tradition and Christians refuse to be held accountable to the community, this mirrors the eclecticism and privatization of faith in the New Age. A second parallel is the anti-intellectual tendency characteristic of New Age and all too common in certain Christian circles as well. Finally, while Christians do not dismiss the physical realm as a dualistic delusion, as much of New Age does, the result is similar when Christians view the physical world as inherently sinful or as an obstacle to salvation.

Positive Aspects of New Age Thought

1. New Age recognizes and gives priority to the spiritual dimension. The New Age movement symbolizes something that is a major frustration for committed atheists. For decades, the atheistic mantra has been that human yearning for the divine would fade and eventually disappear with increased knowledge and technological wizardry. During those years, we have created more creature comforts, cured diseases, streamlined communication, built universities by the thousands and developed amazing new forms of entertainment. Yet only about 5 percent of Americans describe themselves as atheists (although a much higher percentage live as if God doesn't exist).

The New Age movement deserves credit for its recognition that, despite all our wealth, education and technology, our culture is impoverished in matters of meaning, truth, value and transcendence. Thus, New Agers and Christians alike are critical of materialism in both its naturalistic form, which denies the reality of the nonmaterial realm, and its consumerist form, which focuses its energies on the accumulation of material goods to the neglect of spiritual needs and resources. Also, like Christianity, the New Age reminds us that the divine can be missed in everyday life if we are not inclined to look for it.

2. The New Age reminds us of common problems within organized religion. This country is home to millions of people who will say, "I'm not religious, but I'm spiritual." In their stories, you will find countless individuals who have felt victimized or let down by organized religion. The privatized spirituality of New Agers reflects this disenchantment with religious institutions and traditions. Some of this disillusionment grows from social and political conflicts that have used religion, Christianity included, as excuses for warfare and domination. New Age seems like an appealing alternative with its promise of a world without national, religious or ethnic divisions.

On the more individual level, many New Age practitioners have abandoned traditional religions like Christianity because the rules and doctrines seemed oppressive. No doubt, this reflects the desire of some for a have-it-your-way spirituality that makes no demands on them. At the same time, it cannot be denied that churches frequently impose their rules and doctrines in unloving and unforgiving ways. Even in cases where people have not experienced marginalization or exclusion, it is easy to suspect that the faith's true purpose gets lost in all the structures, programming, rules and doctrines of organized religion. Once again, New Age, with its stress on religious experience, its lack of formal structure and its individualized approach, presents an alluring option to many.

There is much here that Christians can applaud and support. Christianity asserts that the heart of faith is a vital relationship with God, not doctrines, creeds, rules and church organization. In contrast to New Age, Christianity believes that the latter are necessary to keep the inner, subjective aspect of faith from slipping into subjectivism (note that subjectivity and subjectivism are two very different things), even though these reinforcing structures are secondary. Still, the New Age stands as a reminder that it is easy to allow the very things that should support an active, inner faith to become a substitute for our relationship with God. Finally, it has, indeed, been the sad case that Christian groups have often adopted narrow and particularistic agendas that have created division and oppression. As we develop in our chapters on postmodern tribalism and nationalism, such agendas forget the universal vision of a Christianity that embraces all people. It is granted that inclusion within Christianity comes with conditions, an idea that the New Age finds exclusive. However, the New Age movement, with its own hierarchy that distinguishes between the spiritually enlightened and the ignorant masses and its own intolerance toward anyone it deems to be intolerant, fails to recognize its own exclusivities.

3. The New Age correctly questions Enlightenment rationality as truth's gatekeeper. While we will argue below that the New Age is too dismissive of rationality, Christians agree that God is incapable of full comprehension by this means. Thus, it reminds us that if we allow rationality to set limits on what can be known or said of God, our view of the divine will be truncated because God transcends reason. If God is not captive to reason, then the New Age is correct in saying that our language about God must leave room for an element of mystery. Much of what we say about the divine must be said indirectly, through symbols and metaphor.

As an illustration, part of this chapter was edited while walking a labyrinth, admittedly a rather unique editing strategy. A labyrinth is related to a maze, but unlike mazes, you do not hit dead-ends from which you must backtrack. Instead, a labyrinth's path leads you to a destination (as long as you keep walking), even though this destination is reached by a circuitous route. To be sure, many things communicated by a labyrinth about our path to and within salvation can also be put into logical language. However the very activity of walking the labyrinth communicates certain truths about our faith in a way that rational language expresses only partially. Thus, while Christianity rejects the anti-intellectualism that permeates the New Age movement, with them we can affirm what every faith tradition throughout history has affirmed—that the divine and our experience of the divine surpass purely logical categories.

POTENTIAL PROBLEMS WITH THE NEW AGE

One way to sum up the root of Christianity's divergences from the New Age is this: the New Age's conviction that "we are gods" puts its worldview on a completely different trajectory than Christianity's belief that "we are God's." They sound the same, and their written forms vary only slightly from each other. Nevertheless, the implications of these minor verbal variations are profound because they reveal quite different understandings of ultimate reality and final authority.

1. The New Age simply replaces the one-sidedness of materialism with a one-sided spiritualism. We have noted our agreement with New Age's rejection of scientific naturalism's materialistic worldview and its desire to acknowledge the presence and primacy of the supernatural. The problem is that New Age does this at the expense of matter. New Age monism, in its claim that "we are gods," even "all is God," turns the material world into a mere illusion, what Hinduism calls *maya*. Christianity clearly parts ways here, arguing that reality is not either God (New Age) or nature (scientific naturalism). Both are reductionistic. Christianity maintains a dualism that distinguishes between God and nature, and ascribes reality, but not equal reality, to both. While God can exist apart from nature, nature (which includes human beings) is the product of God's creative activity and is thus dependent on God. Therefore, nature's dependency means for the Christian that "we are God's."

While we will examine below some of the intellectual incongruities that arise from the idea that "we are gods," we want here to point out the practical difficulties of this view. Life, after all, presents plenty of evidence of our finitude. Regardless of who we are or what our level of enlightenment, our experience tells us that we are limited. Even after achieving god-consciousness, we still have to breathe, sleep, eat, excrete and a host of other physical activities necessary for our survival. We remain limited to occupying one location at a time, still bleed if punctured, and the vast majority of us will have a very difficult time learning trigonometry. If we are deities, we are indeed very peculiar gods. If these types of limitations are false impressions thrust on us by *maya*, they do not appear to be the sorts of illusions that any degree of god-consciousness can eradicate. My Higher Self seems to be stuck with my finite, material, lower self while on this planet.

2. The New Age movement envisions self-salvation. Because the New Age movement clearly gives the supernatural realm primacy over the natural, the quest for salvation is much closer to the surface here than in many other worldviews. However, the New Age understanding of salvation—what we are *saved from, who* is our savior and what we are *saved to*—represents a significant departure from a Christian understanding of salvation.

For New Agers, as we have seen, the hurdle between us and salvation is ignorance. The negative things that diminish life grow out of false impressions, impressions created by dualistic assumptions that split nature from divinity. This is what we must be *saved from*. For the

New Age, the true reality is that all is one, and all is divine. Salvation is escape from the ignorance of our dualistic illusions. Christianity has a different view. Salvation is *salvation from* sin. Our sin is not an illusion, but our real and willful rebellion against the God to whom we belong.

If the New Age is correct that the barrier that keeps us from salvation is only an illusion, then it follows that we are perfectly qualified to be our own savior. To be sure, our thinking is messed up prior to enlightenment, but nothing is wrong with our true, divine self. Thus, our own efforts to cut through our delusional state bring awareness of our own divinity. For Christianity, our being is sinful, so the idea that salvation lies within us is doomed from the start. Christianity differs from New Age in that it confesses the need for a Savior.

Finally, the New Age scheme of salvation says that we are *saved to* ourselves, since "we are gods." Moreover, it must be said that this is a rather narcissistic variant of self-salvation. New Age's eclecticism says that we get to choose which path leads to the Higher Self, and realization of our god-consciousness is verified solely by our own, private experiences. If sin is defined out of existence as only an illusion, no transformation or change in our actions is required. In addition, the New Age does not even submit itself to any of the traditions it professes to admire. It is enamored with eastern monistic thought, but simply chooses what it wants from such traditions as Buddhism or Hinduism. Thus, it accepts monism, reincarnation and mystical enlightenment, but ignores the rigors of self-discipline, chastity, and the social and gender stratification in the traditional forms of these religions.

In sum, when the divine is conceived as an impersonal force, intellect, energy or mind within us, God becomes nothing more than a power source for our own individual purposes. To be fair, many Christians fall into this same trap, envisioning God as a vending machine for health, wealth and other goodies, but this stands in stark contrast to Scripture's view of what we are saved to. Since "we are God's," salvation involves restoration to relationship with the God who has rightful claim over our lives. Such a view of salvation does not allow us to use the divine as a power source for pursuing our goals, but requires a transformation that allows us to become creatures who God works through to accomplish his purposes.

3. The New Age cannot justify its own social agenda. While it refrains from making pronouncements about individual morality, the New Age has, as we have seen, an extremely ambitious agenda for social ethics. We should have little trouble generating enthusiasm for certain elements of their vision. A world without starving children, racial strife, oppression and warfare is an attractive alternative to the present situation. This is a "new" in the New Age that we can be excited about. However, two tough questions lurk in the background of this social agenda. First, can the New Age deliver on its promise for such massive changes and, second, does it even offer any justification for adopting such an agenda?

Concerning the first problem, we have to say that anyone who pays attention to history has little reason for optimism about resolving such massive and long-standing economic, social and political problems. The past is littered with utopian visions that failed miserably, and often simply compounded the old problems. Moreover, the particular fix advocated by New Age, abandonment of dualistic thinking in favor of monism, itself runs afoul of history. One can make a strong case that cultures such as India or China, where monistic thinking prevailed for centuries, have had the least success in solving the type of social problems that the New Age envisions as disappearing under monism. Democracy, equality, elimination of poverty and enhanced health have generally fared better in cultures shaped by dualistic assumptions, although the track record in those places isn't much to boast about either.

The second issue—whether New Age ideas even justify any agenda for social activism—hinges precisely on the monistic worldview. If the distinction between good and evil is nothing but a remnant of dualistic thinking and they are actually one and the same, then why think of starvation and warfare as problems? Why do anything about them at all? Moreover, if the physical realm is an illusion foisted on us by dualistic assumptions, isn't social transformation in the physical world nothing more than a rearrangement of our illusions? We don't actually change anything in the real world because the real world is simply god. We just shuffle our perceptions. But if there is no real difference, why bother?

Coming at it from a different angle, we have to conclude that we are caught in a real mental trap if monism is true. If real evil exists in a world that is also god, then god becomes the problem to be overcome (assuming that evil is a problem), not a means for resolving problems. However, our god-consciousness is supposed to be the motivation for addressing such problems, so that doesn't work out very well. If we suppose that evil is real and we can and should change it, the implications of monism are that we can and do change god when we change the world. If there is no evil, the New Age must admit that its agenda consists of solving nonexistent social problems.

We all want to change the world. However, for all the hype about the New Age's potential for eliminating the travesties of human society, its monistic worldview undercuts either the need or the possibility for doing so. The New Age view of reality either makes evil nonexistent or makes god the cause and embodiment of evil.

4. New Age spirals toward irrationality. We have argued in agreement with the New Age that there is always an element of mystery in God that transcends our rational capacities. Thus, any worldview that seeks to include the divine dimension must operate with a chastened role for human reason. However, there is a significant difference between mystery and absurdity. We fear that the New Age worldview bypasses rather than transcends reason, and thus spirals toward logical absurdity.

In general, New Age thought raises a raft of questions that seem to lead to extremely odd, if not totally absurd, conclusions. Thus, to note just a few examples, if the sole standard of truth is subjective experience, how can we avoid solipsism, the idea that my universe is entirely private and has absolutely no correspondence with the universe that anyone else inhabits? Even more radically, how can we get around the idea that others within my field of consciousness exist only as my personal perception or intuition? If the divine reality that permeates the universe is an impersonal force, how do we become moral, personal and relational beings? Moreover, if the divine is impersonal, why is the only means of verifying divine reality personal and subjective? If we are unaware of our identity as gods, how do we avoid the conclusion that the divine makes mistakes? Does god draw faulty conclusions about god's self?

With minimum thought, you could add to this list of logical absurdities that emerge from the basic premises of the New Age worldview. Our point here is simple, however. The mystical knowledge that "we are gods," the gnosis that New Age claims as its foundation, contradicts logos, the form of thinking that is generally thought of as rational. In contrast, the Christian claim that "we are God's" acknowledges and respects every aspect of God's creation, human reason included. This does not invalidate the idea that there are means of knowing God that transcend reason. Instead, just as God transcends creation while also being its Creator, God transcends reason while also being its source.

CONCLUSION

A friend of mine once went to a Christian conference in a hotel. He wasn't sure about which meeting room he was to go to, but soon found one where a speaker was making a presentation that made generous use of the language of spirituality. After a while, however, he recognized that even though Jesus was frequently referred to in the speaker's words, the spirituality promoted here was not Christian spirituality. Instead, he had mistakenly wandered into a meeting for a New Age group. He left and eventually found the correct room. It turned out, however, that several others who were similarly lost in the hotel stayed through the entire New Age meeting, unaware that it was not the Christian speaker they intended to hear.

One lesson that can be gleaned from this story is that there is considerable overlap between the language and even the practices of Christianity and New Age thought. On the one hand, we should take care not to dismiss certain aspects of Christian practice and language simply because they have New Age parallels, as some Christians do. Meditation and visualization techniques are common within the New Age, but they also have a history in the church that predates the Age of Aquarius by several centuries. Environmentalism is a common characteristic of the New Age movement, but it is not for that reason out of bounds for Christians.

On the other hand, we have tried to make clear that the foundation and goals of Christianity are diametrically opposed to those of the New Age. Thus, Christians do not ground their environmental concern in the idea that trees and rocks are divine. Instead, human beings, made in God's image, are accountable to the God who is the Creator of all things, and thus we cannot treat the world around us carelessly. Christian meditation is not aimed at awareness of our inner divinity, as in the New Age, but at centering our thoughts on a God who is other than us. However, if we are not clear about theological differences between the New Age and Christianity, Christians may believe they are listening to the gospel when they are in fact absorbing the New Age, like those in the hotel who couldn't discern between the two.

Anticipation of a coming new age is not unique to the New Age movement. Since its beginning Christianity has looked forward toward a time when all that degrades life, creates division and throws personal and social peace into turmoil will be destroyed. Christianity's new age, however, is not simply awareness, achieved through self-enlightenment, that "we are gods." Instead, Christians anticipate a new age, brought about by God, in which all acknowledge the lordship of Jesus so that "God may be all in all" (1 Corinthians 15:28). In short, Christianity's new age is one in which the belief that "we are God's" becomes fully realized.

8

POSTMODERN TRIBALISM

My Tribe/My Worldview

I AM UPPER MIDDLE CLASS, HETEROSEXUAL, Caucasian, a male of European descent, educated in the Western tradition and a citizen of the United States. This sentence, spoken in certain settings, would be viewed as a catalog of choices, accomplishments and fortunate circumstances that I should take great pride in. In fact, some would think these attributes, at least the ones I have some control over, represent the pinnacle of human aspiration. In other contexts, however, this sentence reveals my complicity in the oppression of people around the world (to which my high school English teacher would add the sin of adjectival oppression). I would be thought of here as an example of evil rather than a model to emulate. This brings up a point that will be front and center throughout this chapter. Words that describe some of the most fundamental facts about us are not simply brute facts. They have meaning for us, and they mean something, often something very different, to others around us.

The meaning of descriptive adjectives is, of course, incomplete without another factor that we have already hinted at: We live in a world with a great deal of diversity. Thus, millions of people could not find a single description in this chapter's first sentence that fits them once they get past "I am a . . ." The broad array of languages, religions, races, nationalities and other cultural factors reminds us of the global range of diversity.

Cultures have bumped up against each other in the United States since its settlement (and conquest) by those of European descent, and our history has involved significant tension between various groups. However, the frequency and intensity of intercultural interaction has added new variables to an old discussion. Shifting patterns of immigration, twenty-four-hour cable news, the availability of the world through the Internet and the capacity to get to almost any place on the globe in a day (though not necessarily with your luggage) has given today's generation more exposure to worlds beyond their own. New ideas also have been at work, reshaping thoughts about culture. In addition, groups that fall outside traditional cultural definitions have emerged, and press their claims both within and against the dominant social powers. All this has led to a new level of questioning about the place of one's own culture and its interactions with other cultures.

As a result of these shifting trends, young people today come of age with terms like multiculturalism, affirmative action, postmodernism, liberation theology, cultural relativism, postimperialism, ageism, metanarrative, balkanization, identity politics, deconstructionism and culture wars as part of their stock linguistic inventory. On university campuses, they can often major in feminist studies, browse through the bookstore's queer theory section, live in a Hispanic frat or hang out at the Black Student Union. Welcome to the world of postmodern tribalism. However, an upper middle class, heterosexual, Caucasian male of European descent, educated in the Western tradition and a United States citizen—someone like me—might not feel very welcome in any of these places. In fact, I would be excluded from some of these venues.

If I would inquire about my exclusion from majoring in feminist or gay studies or from a Hispanic frat, the first response might be "Join the club. Our history has been full of slammed doors." Fair enough. It's hard to deny a history of extreme limitations on educational prospects and other opportunities for many groups. "But," I might counter, "while this country may not have treated everyone fairly in the past, American ideals provide correctives for those injustices, don't they?" I would be told, "Sure, those ideals work real well, for people like you. But they are interpreted by people who look just like you in ways that ensure that all the power stays in your hands."

Since drawing on American ideals got me nowhere, I might pitch my appeal to something even more basic—human nature. "Isn't there something fundamental to human nature that binds us together and makes exclusion unjust?" The response is twofold. First, I hear, "Human nature is just an abstraction that drains the identity of the socially disempowered. A person's real identity is not found in some general concept of human nature, but in her or his cultural particularity." The second response is something like this: "We have to live most of our lives in a society that is dominated by your (ouch!) culture. If we let you in, you will assume that the rules of your social structures should be followed, and we will be tempted to go along. We need a place that is safe for people like us."

Several things are evident from this hypothetical conversation (which is actually a composite of several conversations). The first and most obvious is a belief that identity is anchored in ethnicity, gender, sexual orientation or some other element. Moreover, it is argued that this particular source of identity has a much stronger pull than general categories such as "American" or even "human being." A third feature is a strong feeling of being a social underdog. Finally, we notice that words I define in one way have very different meanings for them. My language about ideals assumes an appeal to truth that we should all be able to agree on. In contrast, they understand this as language about competition for power. When they talk about the places they see as secure for them, I have to admit that it leaves me feeling less safe. I don't like the idea of being shut out of power structures.

There is a strong emotional undercurrent to the factors above. Both sides of the conversation, whether they speak of it directly or not, express a sense of pain, fear, insecurity, lack of understanding, exclusion and maybe even hostility. The impulse that follows naturally is to find someone "like me," to band together with others who have a similar background. Stated otherwise, this looks like a tribal social structure that many of us thought had been left behind by "civilized" society. Isn't this what tribes do? Tribe members share a powerful sense of identity within a smaller group defined by common language, meaning, experiences and ideas; an awareness of competition with outsiders for scarce resources; and a feeling that the group is necessary for survival. These impulses, combined with features we will discuss below, have led to what we call postmodern tribalism.

FROM MELTING POT TO MULTICULTURALISM TO POSTMODERN TRIBALISM

Whether postmodern tribalism has sufficient parallels to be compared with earlier forms of tribalism is open to debate, but it is obvious that something unprecedented is happening. This newness indicates dissatisfaction with previous ideas about intercultural contact, so before we move on to what we will call postmodern tribalism and explain more directly where the "postmodern" part comes in, we need to know what it is rejecting and why.

The dominant model of cultural interaction throughout the nineteenth and early twentieth centuries in the United States was the idea of the melting pot. This recognized, first off, that our country was a nation of immigrants, especially since those who had been here for centuries were excluded from participation in our national identity. These immigrants all came with cultural, linguistic and ethnic histories. The strength of these histories is evident in that newcomers usually found their first American homes in places like Little Italy, Chinatown or Pennsylvania Dutch country, locations where they found others who shared their heritage.

A generation later, however, children of the first-generation immigrants came to visit their parents in these ethnic enclaves from places like Dallas and Kansas City. As years went on, their grandchildren were buying houses in the suburbs and writing English grammar textbooks, but they could not understand a thing these first-generation immigrants said to each other in their mother tongue. Their Italian, Chinese or German ancestry is still evident in their external appearance, but internally they are cheeseburgers and drive-in movies. The melting pot successfully transformed them from hyphenated American (Italian-American, Asian-American, German-American) to just plain Americans. *E pluribus unum* was not just a national motto; it was a reality. At least for some.

Over time, however, many began to wonder whether they had sacrificed something of significance when they lost whatever had been hyphenated with *American*. Moreover, significant segments of the population were systematically excluded from mainstream society and never had been allowed to become fully American. The latter was felt most keenly by African Americans. This led to a civil rights movement that hit full stride in the 1960s. These twin impulses—concern over loss of cultural identity and exclusion from society—brought about challenges to the "melting pot" metaphor and gave rise to the idea of multiculturalism.

Multiculturalism is a slippery term that means very different things to different people. The definition I intend is probably best captured by a common metaphor—the mosaic. Instead of conceiving of the United States as a place in which former cultural identities eventually gave way to a uniquely American identity, multiculturalism envisioned a nation where cultural identities were maintained, like a piece of tile with its unique features, shapes and colors. When combined, these tiles merged into a coherent, multicolored piece of art. Rather than melting differences away, multiculturalism celebrated cultural variety within a broader unity.

Attempts to move from a melting pot to a mosaic paradigm, not surprisingly, brought strong reactions. This was, after all, a fundamental change in the way the United States thought of itself. Thus, while some saw multiculturalism as burdensome quota systems, others glimpsed an opportunity to right past wrongs. It conjured up positive images of family traditions and a sense of intimate belonging within a shared heritage in certain people; for others it appeared to be unpatriotic and the height of ingratitude toward American culture and opportunities.

Before the debate between the melting pot and the mosaic models was resolved, new voices showed up at the party and radically changed the discussion. One voice, actually a collection of voices, came from those who also felt excluded from power structures, but had been overlooked by multiculturalism. Some were groups defined by ethnicity, such as Hispanics. Others saw themselves as disempowered because of factors such as gender, class, sexual orientation, age and disability. At first glance, it looked like all that was necessary was to add several more colors to the mosaic. However, a second voice, postmodernism, changes all that.

Postmodernism's message is, in part, that all social structures are essentially political in nature. To put it more bluntly, "it's all about power." If that is true, postmodernism said, multiculturalism was doomed to fail because disempowered people had unwittingly bought into the rules of the dominant culture. The ultimate picture formed by the mosaic was already determined by others who used it to preserve their agenda and hang on to power. Thus, postmodernists argued, the oppression of minorities had been aided and abetted by the system's definitions of truth, justice and the American way. How can you find your rightful place in society by appealing to justice when the court systems, the guardians of justice, have systematically denied you the right to vote, attend certain schools or enter high-paying professions? When the truth perpetuated by the creators of the American way portrayed your group as the enemy or simply ignored your contributions, how could this truth—*their* truth—ever become *your* truth? In other words, postmodernism's message is that justice and truth are really words about politics and power. This had the effect of shattering the multicolored mosaic into fragments.

POSTMODERN TRIBALISM

Like the term *multiculturalism*, the word *postmodernism* is dangerous because it has vastly different meanings to different people. Perhaps the best place to start is to take our cue from the *post* in postmodern. Postmodernism sees itself as something opposed to, beyond or after modernism. Thus, just as we cannot fully understand multiculturalism without understanding what they are reacting to—the melting pot—postmodernism only begins to come into focus when we grasp its rejection of modernity.

Modernity, at its root, was the search for absolute certainty. This was not just a matter of my certainty, but a quest for universal truth. Modernists believed that each individual could arrive at this truth if biases were set aside and the proper means of investigation were used. The route to truth went through rational thought, usually understood to be grounded in empirical observation and scientific method. Once harnessed, truth could be put into the service of solving all of our problems, since problems resulted from believing untrue ideas. Whatever vestiges of error that remained from tribal superstition, the ideas of particular cultures or beliefs that could not be confirmed by observation—in short, illogical ideas—had to be uprooted, satirized into submission, corrected through proper education or marginalized. In other words, beliefs that did not conform to modernism's standards of logic had to be conquered.

*Post*modernism finds every one of these modernist aims—universality, certainty, absolute truth, individualism, unbiased neutrality, rationality, confidence in science, conquest—problematic. Many who seek a common point of departure for postmodernism look to the statement of Jean-François Lyotard, who said, "I define *postmodern* as incredulity towards metanarratives."[1] A metanarrative is a story that transcends any individual or cultural narrative. It is a grand deposit of truth which, if grasped, makes sense of our origins, explains what is right and good and defines our purpose for existence. Thus, the melting pot concept is viewed as a modernist metanarrative that says that all particular cultural expressions should give way to the truth of the American way. Often this metanarrative has maintained that we should export this eternal truth to other parts of the world in the form of democracy and equality for all or in the benefits of global capitalism. We can also hear the sounds of modernist metanarrative in some of the worldviews we examine in this book, such as naturalism, consumerism or individualism.

---

[1]Jean-François Lyotard, *The Postmodern Condition: A Report on Knowledge*, trans. Geoff Bennington and Brian Massumi (Minneapolis: University of Minnesota Press, 1984), p. xxiv.

Postmodernism looks at universal stories, claims to absolute truth and ideas of unbiased neutrality with disbelief. While modernism rejects cultural particularities and seeks to absorb unique practices into something that is more universal (e.g., human nature), postmodernism elevates particularity. No one is just an individual or primarily a member of the human race. We are born with specific skin pigmentation and genetic characteristics. We land in a world where a particular language, nationality, religion, tradition and heritage are already there waiting for us. These factors, and others, make us part of a group with its own identity and history. No one gets a choice in this matter. Thus, it is not through abstract concepts like human nature that we discover who we are. Our concrete realities—our history, gender and all the other particular factors—give us our roots, a sense of belonging and identity in a chaotic world. Sever those roots and we lose something crucial to our identity.

Some postmodern thinkers attribute a power to this cultural pull that is almost deterministic; others are content to state only that it is highly influential. To some degree or another, however, postmodernists assert we all carry a significant amount of cultural baggage, and that baggage informs our understanding of how we should respond to cultures other than our own. Stated otherwise, what we believe to be good, true or purposeful cannot be divorced from how our tribe sees the world and its place within it. Thus, the subplot of cultural interaction has a social dimension we cannot overlook. We never come into the world as colorless, genderless, ahistorical individuals. Our ideas and identity are intimately linked with the actual particularities of our lives, not the universal abstractions of modernism.

POSTMODERN TRIBALISM AND POWER

Another dimension of intercultural interaction is that not every tribe has equal power. While certain forms of power are obvious, such as the military defeat of one tribe by another, others are less overt. In particular, postmodernism focuses on the role of social status in our interpretations of what counts as real, good and true. Thus, for example, a powerful tribe like white Christian America might interpret the exodus story in Scripture as a historical event that anticipates our salvation from enslavement to sin. A tribe that perceives itself as disempowered, such as African Americans, may read the exodus story as a hopeful vision of something yet to come for them. Rather than anticipating a spiritualized liberation from the immaterial powers of sin, the exodus narrative is interpreted as liberation from economic, political and social slavery.

We cannot help but notice that, while both groups look back to the same story and find the same motifs of slavery and freedom within it, the meaning of those themes is shaped by cultural experience. White interpreters might find the African American take on the exodus narrative baffling. No one in this country is enslaved, and salvation is understood "by everyone" as something that transcends political or economic categories. African Americans would argue that the most effective ownership of other human beings is not necessarily enslavement. Whoever makes the rules about ownership, justice, education and what counts as salvation controls everything and everyone. Thus, they would say that the poor throughout history have been kept down precisely because spiritualized definitions of salvation allow the haves to keep the have-nots down.

This leads to another important concept in postmodernism—incommensurability. Incommensurability means that things that appear on the surface to be equal assume completely different meanings in different contexts. "Pharaoh," for white readers of the exodus story, is the power of sin; justice is freedom from this power, with a significant level of punishment for Pharaoh and the pursuing Egyptians thrown in for good measure. For African American, gays or South Americans, "Pharaoh" may well refer to the white readers, and justice means spoiling the wealth of the Egyptians to get what is due them. In short, we can't even agree on who the "good guys" and "bad guys" are in the story. Incommensurability, then, means that the exodus story is not a single story at all. What it *means* depends on the social context in which it is read, regardless of what it *meant* to the original author (who wrote out of a social situation that no modern reader shares).

Disagreements about how one interprets the exodus narrative remind us of the pivotal role religion has played in shaping ideas about our identity. The fact that Christianity presents itself as a metanarrative, a story that explains our place in the universe, helps us understand the hostility directed at it by some proponents of postmodernism. The complaint is that Christianity's claims to possess universal truth have been used by the dominant culture to erase particularity and conquer enemies. In this view, then, if one is to resist existing power arrangements, it must also reject Christianity. The result has been that the social influence once possessed by Christianity in this country has been challenged. Christians have often reacted against this social marginalization with their own form of tribalism, creating a subculture with its own vocabulary, music, literature and educational system, much of which expresses this sense of being a cultural outsider.

SUMMARY

Modernism views one's sexual orientation, gender and race as contingent properties. It acknowledges, for example, that human beings come in male and female genders, but says that one's gender does not determine one's humanness. It is thus a contingent property of humans; you can be one whether you are female or male. For postmodern tribalism, however, humanness cannot be abstracted from gender or any other particularity of our lives. These are not contingent properties, but are instead essential to our ideas of identity, morality, religion and truth.

Emphasizing particularity over universality yields significant implications. First, it means that truth does not come in a one-size-fits-all variety but is, instead, socially constructed. What we take to be truth will be shaped by our gender, history, culture, race, abilities or sexual orientation. Second, one's sense of well-being cannot be measured by any supposed universal standard, but is determined by how well one is integrated into a tribe with its unique ideas of the true, the good and the beautiful. If this is the case, the third implication of postmodern tribalism is that marginalized groups must undermine the claims of dominant culture in order to get the social recognition and power that is due them. If everything is politics, political strategies (understood broadly) must be used to bring about a shift in the power structures.

POSITIVES OF POSTMODERN TRIBALISM

In some segments of Christianity, postmodernism is the symbol of all that is wrong with the world today. To be sure, tensions exist in versions of postmodernism that reject Christianity as a metanarrative to define our essential problem, offer a route to salvation and grant meaning to life. In reaction, many Christians retreat to modernism, consciously or not, with its promise of universal, absolute truth. However, modernism has often appealed to the individual, the nation, science or human reason in general as the foundation for absolute truth and has relegated God to the periphery, which makes it a questionable intellectual home for Christianity. In other words, if modernism was completely hospitable to Christianity, this book would not contain chapters about individualism, nationalism or naturalism, all worldviews that arose with modernism. Thus, even if postmodern tribalism is unacceptable as a Christian worldview, it offers a useful appraisal of modernism. After all, this is fundamentally what *post*modernism is about—a critique of modernity.

1. Postmodern tribalism can help us develop empathy. Certain segments of American Christianity today once felt very comfortable within the mainstream of American society. Over the years, though, civil rights crusades, multiculturalism, the emergence of postmodern tribalism and other factors have brought significant changes that many Christians believe have placed them on the outside of social structures. Public schools sponsor "holiday" programs that don't mention Christmas but put Kwanzaa and Hanukkah front and center, universities give preference in admissions to certain minority groups and Disneyland advertises "gay day" at its parks.

Our interest here is not whether these developments are positive or negative, but to gauge Christian reaction. One common response is to find a place where people still share our ideas and understandings about what the real social problems and solutions are. In short, when we feel pushed out, we start looking for like-minded people to "tribe" with. We often use the term *fellowship* as a euphemism, but if our reaction is rooted in fear, tribalism is a better description. Instead of withdrawing into our tribe, however, a sense of marginalization can provide a greater sense of empathy for others who also feel left out. The latter clearly seems to be a more Christian response.

If we have to fight the impulse to withdraw into the safety of our group, the sense of disempowerment others experience and their own tribalistic responses make a lot more sense to us. Power can blind us to the oppression of others, which makes it difficult to feel empathy. To those in power, pleas from those on the fringes of society sound like whining. But if you are on the fringe yourself, these pleas make much more sense. To this extent, then, sharing this sense of disempowerment might help American Christians hear what others have been trying to say. This holds the possibility of rediscovering our obligation to social justice.

2. Tribalism can help Christians recognize dependence on alien definitions of power. Christians have struggled for centuries to balance our place in God's kingdom with our place in society. When Emperor Constantine gave favored status to the Christian religion in A.D. 313, it brought significant changes in the relationship between Christianity and the state. While it brought an end to the persecution of Christians and facilitated significant numerical growth, many trace the demise of the early church's spiritual vitality to this event. The problem is that when Christians gain different forms of social influence (e.g., economic, political, educational), we tend to get them tangled up and confused with spiritual forms of authority. Unless one is careful, spiritual resources can be co-opted by social power and we can become dependent on the latter for our sense of well-being.

Postmodernism views the world as competition for social power to advance the cause of one's own group. This confronts Christians with an important choice. Do we buy into this definition of power and want to do all we can to protect our share of it, or do we pursue a uniquely Christian understanding of authority? Many long for a return to "the good old days" when Christianity had a great deal of influence within the corridors of power. Others, however, see great danger for Christianity when those who hold secular forms of power wrap it with spiritual language. We don't want to get mired down in the complex discussion of how Christians should deal with our relationships to social power structures, but it seems clear that overreliance and misuse of secular authority threatens to sap our spiritual vitality.

3. Tribalism can help Christians recognize the systemic aspect of sin. Christians often fall into the trap of limiting sin to the individual level. However, sin has a history that becomes ingrained in our social structures. Economic factors made it difficult to confront the evils of slavery; longstanding ideas about intellectual superiority perpetuated colonialism and sexism; and a sense of Manifest Destiny made it possible to dehumanize Native Americans in the drive to expand this country's borders. In these and too many other dark chapters in our history, sincere, well-meaning and bright Christians have participated in the systems that supported oppression, and Christianity's reputation has suffered greatly as a result. Entanglement in systematic evil generally does not arise because of the evil motives of individuals, but because social systems are so deeply embedded in our ways of thinking and acting.

This helps us understand tribalism's focus on the power of systems and cultures. A legal or economic structure that seems natural and fair from one cultural perspective can appear alien and oppressive from a different cultural outlook. When we listen to voices from outside our own "tribe," we discover places where, often unconsciously, we have perpetuated power imbalances. While tribalism gravitates toward addressing these inequities from the safety of one's own cultural perspective, Christianity's claim to our primary loyalty requires us to constantly evaluate and critique the power structures around us, especially when we gain certain benefits from these systems. However, a critical part of that evaluation requires consciousness about how these social systems strip others of dignity and rights. Tribalism has been helpful in creating this consciousness.

4. Culture provides a way of ordering life. When a person dies, there is a universal expectation that the deceased's loved ones will exhibit proper respect in the way they say farewell. This is only one of many basic life functions that people everywhere have had to fulfill. We form families, educate children, create governments, punish lawbreakers, worship, celebrate important benchmarks in lives and produce goods, in addition to memorializing our dead. In short, *what* we do across cultures is universal. *How* we do this, on the other hand, is shaped by culture, and every culture will have different practices. The ways we perform these universal functions in life are not insignificant, because they give us a sense of being at home in the universe. They bring an order and rhythm to life and provide a framework through which we express the importance we attach to these fundamental activities.

Variations in practices, rituals and customs between cultures create tension, however, because what seems normal to insiders will seem quite alien, and even downright wrong, to cultural outsiders. When faced with this tension, modernism's inclination is to see cultural variations as deviations that should be brought into conformity with universal truth. Postmodern tribalism, on the other hand, encourages the preservation of diversity, because it recognizes that these practices give structure to life's fundamental functions.

To a large extent, Christians can applaud postmodern tribalism's acceptance of a diverse range of customs, because many of these, in themselves, are morally neutral. Thus, when a loved one dies, whether we bury the body, cremate it, shroud it and carry it through the streets to a burial site, or place it in a stone crypt, most people will not feel compelled to judge different funerary rites in moral terms. That is not to say, however, that they are culturally neutral. From my cultural perspective, it would be quite uncomfortable to have the mortal remains of a loved one carried through a public street in a funeral procession. We do not intend to say that all the ideas attached to funeral rites, or any other basic human activity, are of equal value, and this is where we will part ways with postmodern tribalism later in this chapter. Our point is that *how* we express our sorrow for departed family members, worship God or provide nurture for our children will be shaped, in large part, by culture. Respecting such deeply embedded practices is an important aspect of respect for all people, a value that Christians should find natural.

POTENTIAL PROBLEMS WITH POSTMODERN TRIBALISM

How we get along with people of different religions, races, lifestyles and nationalities is one of the most pressing issues of the age. The interests of postmodern tribalism and Christianity merge in the desire for mutual respect between cultures and a rejection of domination of marginalized groups by imperialistic power. However, Christians must ask whether a tribalist worldview has sufficient resources to reach, or even to justify, such goals. It states that it wants all voices to be heard, but do the assumptions of postmodern tribalism provide a basis for real communication? While they advocate respect for all people of all cultures, does their intellectual foundation justify this respect? When postmodern tribalism eliminates truth as a final authority, can it avoid defaulting to power as the means for its actions and beliefs? Finally, can we find any justification within this worldview for overcoming oppression?

1. Postmodern tribalism often assumes cultural determinism. The belief that our perceptions of time, ethics, the sacred, death and a host of other things always comes to us through the filter of culture is central to postmodern tribalism. In its stronger forms, it states that culture *determines* our perceptions of reality; in fact, our understanding of the world cannot be other than it is. However, when we look at the broad divergence in cultural ideas and practices, the implications of cultural determinism are quite frightening. If true, we would never really be able to understand motivations, express empathy or share beliefs with anyone from outside our limited culture and era. If our nature is nothing but the product of tribal variables that are incomprehensible outside that context, we can only gaze at others from across the cultural abyss and scratch our heads in bewilderment.

Yet if we look closely, postmodern tribalism must appeal to commonalities in human nature to communicate its beliefs. If one tribe's views about violence, oppression and marginalization are nothing other than their unique perspective, a perspective that is not duplicated in any other group, then are these views intelligible to anyone else? Outsiders may hear the words, but words are not the same as meanings. If postmodern tribalism is correct about cultural determinism, an individual can never attach the same meanings to language by another individual who is outside his or her own group.

Our practical experience with intercultural interaction seems to indicate that we do share common turf with others that allows for communication. While we may lack an intimate understanding of the linguistic nuances, traditions, history or intellectual legacies behind the educational structures, legal systems or family configurations of a different culture, there is something within our shared human nature that allows us to understand another culture's impulse to educate their populace, promote justice and raise children in a safe and loving environment. Thus, postmodern tribalism is right in recognizing that cultural differences create some obstacles in communication. However, it overstates the case by making our backgrounds deterministic, and thus cannot explain how crosscultural communication is even possible.

2. Postmodern tribalism relativizes "tribes" while absolutizing "my tribe." Even if postmodern tribalism could explain how diverse cultural groups can communicate ideas across tribal boundaries, it offers no common authority to enact its agenda of peaceful coexistence between the broad range of racial, ethnic, religious and lifestyle groups. This should be viewed as tragic by Christians, because we agree with the critique that modernism has allowed certain cultures to use beliefs that were thought to be objective, universal and eternal to subjugate minority voices and shut them out of power structures. After all, Christians must reject the belief that any set of cultural truths, norms, traditions or customs carries final authority. Moreover, Christians have often felt marginalized under the assumptions of modernism. For example, modernists argued that a religion like Christianity, based on divine revelation, had no business in universities that valued science and reason—ideas that scientific naturalists viewed as eternally and universally valid for all people. Thus, when postmodernism challenged modernist assumptions about the adequacy of reason, as defined by this one particular subculture, there was no longer any justification for excluding Christians, or any other group, from any conversation.

This should seem like good news for Christianity for two reasons. First, Christians should certainly hope that previously suppressed voices are heard in our social and political conversations. Second, it is also natural for Christians to think their views should be taken seriously. This "good news" quickly evaporated for Christians, however, because when postmodern tribalism rejected universal reason as authoritative, it filled this vacuum with the authority of *one's own* tribal norms and cultural customs. As we have seen above, postmodern tribalism asserts that there are multiple truths. And because my tribe is determinative of what I perceive as true, the beliefs and power structures of my tribe become authoritative for me, even if not for those outside the tribe.

This leads to several seemingly insurmountable problems. First, if our culture is both determinative and authoritative for us, it makes it difficult to see *how* one could have any way to critique or correct one's own culture. If our perception of reality is so socially determined that we cannot escape it, we have no way to stand apart from it, a requirement for evaluating something. After all, the culture we evaluate, if it is our own, is also the standard for evaluating culture.

It also leaves us unable to explain *why* one would ever critique or change anything within one's culture. Thus, if my tribe practices female genital mutilation, such practices are the truth of my culturally constructed reality. How or why, then, could an individual within this society argue that it would be *better* to prohibit the practice of female genital mutilation? To make such an argument, you have to go outside current cultural practices to find a standard of comparison to determine what is better, which postmodern tribalism deems impossible. In the end, when tribalism absolutizes culture's determinative power over an individual, this puts culture in the place of God. One's entire concept of reality, morality, salvation, origin and purpose ultimately depends on one's tribal traditions, not a transcendent God.

Second, replacing some supposed eternal truth with the "truth" advocated by my own tribe does not guarantee respect or even toleration for outsiders. That is clearly evident from our world today, where some cultural norms demand subjugation or death for those who do not conform to the standards that the group would impose on those outsiders if they were so empowered. Thus, rather than providing a foundation for respect, absolutizing our own culture trivializes the beliefs of others. We may not feel the compulsion to conquer or kill outsiders, but there is no reason to expect that anyone else should pay any attention to your statements since they carry no authority outside your tribe.

3. Postmodern tribalism degenerates into just another power play. How one defines a problem makes a great deal of difference in what one sees as the solution. Modernism, for better or worse, defined our basic problem as ignorance that could be eliminated by knowing the truth. Postmodern tribalism rejects this, arguing that modernism used truth as a smoke screen to conceal its actual goal—attaining power. Postmodern tribalism wants to rectify the power imbalances perpetuated by modernism but says that we cannot appeal to universal truth to do this. So how do we achieve this end? Without some common truth or virtue as justification for correcting long-standing wrongs, the only means that postmodern tribalism has for rectifying unfair power arrangements would be power itself.

Postmodern tribalism's reliance on power to achieve its ends has several unfortunate implications. First, it involves a reductionistic view of human nature. We want to avoid the impression that our economic or social standings are unimportant to our well-being. We are social, economic and political beings, but we are not *just* that. Thus, when postmodern tribalism defines the human problem in purely social or economic terms, it overlooks other important dimensions of human nature and will thus assume that my status is defined entirely by the social well-being of my particular tribe.

Second, there is irony in postmodern tribalism's reliance on power as the means of obtaining the ends sought by one's tribe. After all, its fundamental critique of modernism is its use of truth to justify coercion against other groups. The problem in postmodern tribalism is that, if maximizing the power of my own group with its own particular truth is my sole goal, what prevents me from using coercive force to achieve such goals for my own group? If "it's all about power," and the only forms of power recognized are social or economic, then use of force to attain these goals for my own group is not just permissible, but a moral duty. The irony, then, is that this becomes a recipe for heightening tribal animosity, inequality and strife rather than eliminating it.

4. Postmodern tribalism creates a culture (and cult) of victimhood. An interesting feature of postmodern tribalism is that many groups use their status as victims as a means to stake their claim to resources of power. On the one hand, we don't want to belittle legitimate claims to victimization. Rectifying systems and situations that cause harm to people is a fundamental goal of moral behavior. On the other hand, the tribalistic approach to victimization creates several problems. First, no incentive exists for tribes to overcome oppression if that is the very thing they rely on to claim a right to the power they lack. This is made even more difficult by postmodern tribalism's tendency to view victimhood as conferring moral virtue on those who are oppressed. If victims are good and the powerful are inherently corrupt, success in gaining social power then puts them on the side of the oppressor. Moreover, if claims to victimhood gain force according to the degree one suffers, it creates an odd competition between tribes to be the most oppressed. Lack of power makes a person a winner in this contest. The result is that postmodern tribalism sends mixed signals that offer a strong incentive to exaggerate and perpetuate claims to victimhood and overlook real signs of progress in correcting past wrongs. True suffering is a horrific thing and should never be trivialized. However, postmodern tribalism is susceptible to using suffering as a political and social lever without offering any foundation for eliminating it.

5. Postmodern tribalism is culturally reductionistic. Terms like *tribe* or *culture* are not quite as simple as they sound, because they include so many elements—language, history, traditions, religion, ethnic, racial and other components. However, tribalism, as often practiced, tends to be selective about which cultural element really "counts." Thus, it often arbitrarily picks out one feature of an individual's background—for example, sexual orientation, gender, ethnicity or economic class—and reduces a person's identity to that factor.

We quickly recognize the problem with this reductionism if we return to examine some of the adjectives I used to describe myself at the beginning of the chapter—upper middle class, heterosexual, Caucasian, a male of European descent, educated in the Western tradition and a citizen of the United States. "Upper middle class" is not the cultural equivalent of "heterosexual." "Caucasian" is not the same as "U.S. citizen." In fact, none of these terms describes the same thing about me. Moreover, this does not tell my entire cultural story, which would also have to include things such as my rural, blue-collar, Kansas upbringing. So which of these cultural factors determines my tribal obligations? In short, the reduction of our identity to one factor among many is completely arbitrary and does not do justice to actual human beings.

CONCLUSION

If we have done an adequate job of communicating our position to this point, a couple of things should be clear. First, we agree with much of tribalism's critique of modernism. The latter has often used coercive measures to bring different cultures into conformity with a dominant culture that claims to be the sole guardian of truth. Modernism has often contributed to strife between groups and has failed to recognize the significant ways in which culture shapes our view of the world. At the same time, it should also be clear that we are pessimistic about postmodern tribalism's claim to have the answer for these problems. We think that Christianity offers a third option.

Christianity was born in a context in which people of different languages, ethnic backgrounds and religious sympathies were in close proximity, and those people had to make some important choices about how to deal with tribal loyalties. Christianity's response stands in contrast to modernism's attempt to level off all cultural differences and postmodernism's quest to absolutize the tribe. On the one hand, when Paul proclaims, "There is neither Jew nor Greek, slave nor free, male nor female, for you are all one in Christ Jesus" (Galatians 3:28), he points to Jesus as the reality that binds all together and transcends our religious, ethnic, economic, political or gender identities. No cultural factor could ever hold ultimate authority for us. On the other hand, when the earliest Christians were confronted with the question of whether Gentile converts would have to be circumcised, an extremely important cultural symbol and practice for Jewish Christians, they concluded that "we should not make it difficult for the Gentiles who are turning to God" (Acts 15:19), by imposing a culturally alien practice on them. In short, they were able to distinguish between a cultural means of expressing faith in God and faith in God itself.

Perhaps the place where this picture comes together most vividly is in Revelation, where we see "a great multitude that no one could count, from every nation, tribe, people and language, standing before the throne and in front of the Lamb. . . . And they cried out in a loud voice: 'Salvation belongs to our God, who sits on the throne, and to the Lamb'" (Revelation 7:9-10). In this vision, we see the ultimate episode of a grand Christian metanarrative that stretches from creation, Fall and redemption, and it culminates in this glorious vision of God. To the extent that it is a metanarrative, it contradicts postmodern tribalism's view that no overarching story of the world is universally true. However, we should not overlook the fact that this worship of God occurs, not apart from, but within the context of different nations, tribes, peoples and languages. Within this passage, people retain their identity as members of specific nations, tribes and language groups while, at the same time, addressing their worship toward the same God.

I am upper middle class, heterosexual, Caucasian, a male of European descent, educated in the Western tradition and a citizen of the United States. These factors provide some insight into how I live and view the world. However, the fact that I am also a Christian requires that none of these should ever be ultimately authoritative. When I am surrounded by folks who use other adjectives to describe their cultural particularities, it reminds me that, while God transcends the unique features of any tribe, the way we experience God and express our faith will always be shaped by our time and place in the world.

9

SALVATION BY THERAPY

Not as Good as It Gets

At a pivotal point in the movie *As Good as It Gets,* Jack Nicholson's character walks into a roomful of people waiting to see their psychiatrist and yells, "What if this is as good as it gets?" His cynical outburst, which suggests that therapy offers little hope to those seeking healing, would certainly have a jarring effect in that context. After all, the people are in the counselor's waiting room precisely because they believe that when life isn't good, therapy will help things get better.

They are not alone. We humans are a hopeful species. Most of us will not let ourselves believe that a psychologically wounded life is as good as it can get. In this chapter, we will maintain that hopeful stance and assume that our social and psychological injuries can be made better. The question we want to ask is why the people in *As Good as It Gets,* and in huge numbers throughout our culture, expect life to get better *there.* Why the therapist?

If that question—why the therapist?—sounds odd to you, it will be helpful to put it in historical context. People have always had the sorts of problems that we now almost automatically take to therapists. However, until about a century ago, behavioral specialists such as counselors, psychologists and psychiatrists did not exist. Where did people prior to the twentieth century take their problems? Chances are, if they took them anywhere, people would have discussed issues of this nature with religious leaders. This represents a major shift because, in the past century, the Western world has become what Philip Reiff famously refers to as a "therapeutic culture." In this shift to a therapeutic culture, the therapist has replaced the pastor or priest as the professional person to look to for relational or behavioral assistance.

The displacement of religious professionals by therapists is noteworthy in itself, but the speed with which the ascendancy of the therapist has occurred is remarkable. For centuries, religion was almost universally viewed as the refuge of first resort. In contrast, psychology is a newcomer in historical terms. Yet its authority is now firmly entrenched in Western society. When people feel that life is not what it should be, they consult their psychologist, not their clergyperson (if they even have one). If an employee struggles with addiction problems that interfere with work, they are sent to counselors. Such is the case as well when people seek help with family or marriage problems. If a television station or the courts need an expert to make sense of the mind and motivations of a serial killer or pedophile, the mental health professional comes up first in their rolodex. Advice is solicited from the therapist on child-rearing, depression, adjustment to divorce, crisis management following a natural disaster or traumatic experience, and a host of other problems that stand between us and a life that is as good as it gets.

It's All About Salvation

Millions of people today view therapy as a means, and some view it as *the* means, to a good life. If the language about the good life parallels what we mean when we talk about salvation, this explains why we have included a chapter about salvation by therapy in a book about worldviews. It isn't just the case, as we have pointed out above, that many roles previously played by the clergy, a profession focused on salvation, have now been assumed by therapists. The prevalence of therapy tells us something about the pursuit of salvation—we have this inkling that our lives are not yet as good as they can get or should get. This represents a discontent with a partial life and a desire to pursue fullness.

Assuming that we do feel this need to pursue a more complete life, a big question that needs to be addressed is how much faith we should invest in modern psychology to help us reach this goal. Does it, in the end, hinder our pursuit of an abundant life? Does psychology offer the best and perhaps the only reliable means for dealing with personal and relational problems? Is the answer somewhere between these extremes?

THREE VIEWS OF PSYCHOLOGY AND CHRISTIANITY

A segment of the Christian world believes that psychology is detrimental to one's spiritual and mental health. This position, often going under the name of biblical counseling, argues that the Bible should be the sole source for guidance by pastoral counselors. In Stanton Jones and Richard Butman's book, *Modern Psychotherapies*, one of the authors recalls a conversation with a prominent figure in the biblical counseling movement. Asked if he had any advice for Christians studying psychology, this counselor's response was, "Drop out of graduate school. If you want to serve God as a counselor, you can only do so by going to seminary, studying the Word of God rather than the words of men, and becoming a pastor."[1] The assumption behind this advice is that all problems are spiritual in nature and should be dealt with by means of spiritual tools.

This response, in part, reflects concerns about certain tensions between convictions found in some psychological systems and basic Christian beliefs. We share many of those concerns and will highlight some of those worldview clashes below. However, we part ways with the biblical counseling movement on a crucial point. We disagree with their contention that modern psychological research and methodologies provide no insight beyond what is available from Scripture. While the Bible is a trustworthy and invaluable source for understanding human psychology and relationships, it is not an exhaustive compendium of such knowledge.

---

[1]Stanton L. Jones and Richard E. Butman, *Modern Psychotherapies* (Downers Grove, Ill.: Inter-Varsity Press, 1991), p. 18.

While we disagree with those who find no valid role for psychology in resolving social and behavioral problems, we find the other extreme of the spectrum equally troubling. This position, which we refer to as "salvation by therapy," is reductionistic in the opposite way. Instead of defining all psychological difficulties as a form of spiritual failure or maladjustment, as the biblical counseling school does, salvation by therapy reduces spiritual problems out of existence by defining them as exclusively psychological in nature.

The reduction of all problems, including those that are spiritual in nature, to matters of psychological maladjustment is what distinguishes salvation by therapy from psychology in general. The latter views psychology as a tool that can be integrated into a Christian worldview. Salvation by therapy, by contrast, is an absolutist position that offers its worldview as an alternative to religion. Thus, no theological view of the universe is seen as compatible. Instead, attributing anything at all to the spiritual realm is viewed as a symptom of mental illness or arrested psychological development rather than as a potential ally in the healing process. Salvation by therapy rejects the spiritual dimension altogether; thus theological resources have no therapeutic value because they misdiagnose psychological difficulties as spiritual problems. Only when we see psychological and behavioral problems for what they are—purely and exclusively psychological issues—can we have any hope for improving the lives of clients who are burdened with such difficulties.

Our position lies between these extremes. On the one hand, we reject the biblical counseling perspective because it is reductionistic. To be sure, Scripture supplies all-important information about what a healthy life or marriage should look like. However, it doesn't delve into the particulars about processes for restoring individuals and couples to psychological or relational wholeness any more than it offers guidelines for performing gallbladder surgery. On the other hand, we find it similarly reductionistic to believe that psychological or relational discord has no spiritual significance, as is the case in salvation by therapy. Instead, we find psychology a useful but incomplete discipline, whose research and treatment regimens should be integrated into a full-bodied quest for the abundant life.

Modern Psychology and Its Roots

Psychology, literally translated, means the study of the *psyche*, the soul. In this traditional sense, it is the study of the human being's interior mental life—our motivations, thoughts, emotions, spiritual sensitivities and moral impulses. Under this definition, then, psychology has deep historical roots. Prior to its emergence in the early twentieth century as an independent university discipline, it existed (and still exists) as a subset of philosophy and theology.

The idea of psychology as a systematic study of the soul is pivotal because early thinkers generally agreed that the *psyche* is what distinguishes human beings from animals. Even though human beings often eat the same things as nonhumans, possess the same organs, die of the same diseases and share numerous other biological similarities, the *psyche's* capacities set the human being apart. These differences, then, mark the boundaries between biology, which we share with animals, and psychology, which humans alone possess. Though disagreements raged about the nature of the soul or even whether it was a separate human component that existed in distinction from our bodies, early psychology agreed that human beings are a breed apart with capacities that transcend those of other biological creatures.

Psychology in this more traditional sense still exists today, but the professions we normally associate with the term began to take shape in the late nineteenth and early twentieth centuries. At this time, discovery within the natural sciences experienced explosive growth. Some who were deeply interested in human social and psychological behavior began to ask whether their own investigations might experience similar breakthroughs if they applied methods similar to those used by the natural sciences. As this methodological shift took hold, the social sciences came into their own as disciplines distinct from theology and philosophy. The goal of this new form of psychology, then, was to attain knowledge about human beings that was testable, quantifiable and observable. In short, the social science approach says that psychological knowledge should be confirmed in a manner that parallels the natural sciences' verification processes.

The shift to a scientific method of verification generates a decisive question. Should this modern, scientific approach to psychology *replace* the older view, or does it provide tools that *supplement* prior perspectives? This question arises because methods are not simply neutral tools. Tools are adapted for particular types of jobs. The issue is whether the scientific method is the proper tool for investigating the full scope of human existence and activity. Can the assumptions underlying a scientific approach to psychology offer answers about the goal of human life or what constitutes psychological well-being or health?

If the answer to the question above is yes, we are dealing with salvation by therapy, which views scientific psychology as a *replacement* for philosophical and theological approaches. While prescientific perspectives assumed realities that could not be directly observed or measured, this understanding of psychology rejects immaterial entities such as God or the soul (a bit ironic for a discipline that means "the study of the soul"). Thus, it argues that psychology should eliminate the distinction between the human and the nonhuman realms. Differences between nonhuman and human behaviors (language, aesthetic judgment, morality, spiritual sensitivity, etc.) arise only because of greater complexity in the human world, not because of unique human capacities. The insights of psychology are not simply a partial explanation for ourselves and our world, but provide a complete worldview (generally a variation of scientific naturalism) that competes against the philosophical or theological worldviews it seeks to replace.

In contrast, many have a more modest view of psychology's reach. While scientific study of the human being provides insight into human nature, our problems and how to seek healing, it also maintains that certain aspects of our existence stand outside the scope of science and its tools. For example, these people could agree with the first camp that scientific research confirms that the use of certain drugs by pregnant women can result in neurological problems for children, and that some behavioral disorders common to such children are linked to these neurological issues. Nevertheless, this psychological approach argues that this is not the complete story. We cannot reduce all human behavior to biological causes nor can all the answers be found in science's toolkit. Psychology must recognize "soulish" human capacities such as reasoning, choosing, desiring, loving or worshiping as having a connection with our biology, but are not fully comprehensible in those terms alone.

Moreover, those who embrace a "modest psychology" argue that science is a great descriptive tool but is incomplete as a prescriptive instrument. It can describe, for example, the causal connections between certain drugs and the resulting behaviors. It may even be helpful in a prescriptive sense by suggesting certain therapies as effective means toward healthy behaviors and attitudes. However, psychology itself lacks the ability to determine whether certain behaviors should be identified as healthy or abnormal. Similarly, scientific tools provide insight into why people believe in certain things or act in certain ways, but it cannot tell us what we *should* believe or how we *should* act. In order to offer distinctions such as normal or abnormal, healthy or unhealthy, this mediating view asserts that psychology must recognize its limitations and rely on tools that supplement and go beyond those provided by the natural sciences.

DIFFERENT SCHOOLS

We have sketched out two distinct views of the scope of psychology above—salvation by therapy, which offers itself as an all-inclusive worldview, and a more modest psychology, which can be integrated into a variety of other worldviews. However, our discussion of psychology's proper scope touches on only one part of our task. The last century has seen the development of a broad array of psychological theories. Some of them, because of their assumptions, fall into the salvation by therapy category by offering a totalizing worldview; others fit into a "modest psychology" view.

It falls outside the margins of this chapter to attempt a comprehensive survey of psychological theories. We will, instead, limit our examination to four representative approaches—Freud's psychoanalytic theory, Rogers's person-centered therapy, Skinner's behaviorism and family-systems therapy. Even within this small sampling, we will find fundamental disagreements in their analyses of the human situation and their prescriptions for it, and these divergences would be multiplied in a more comprehensive survey. In addition, much vital information will be missing from the approaches examined because of space limitations, so our view of each provides only some fundamental ideas.

FREUD AND PSYCHOANALYSIS

One school that exemplifies the salvation by therapy worldview originates in Sigmund Freud's (1856-1939) thought. He presents his therapeutic approach, psychoanalysis, as more than a means helping people navigate life's mazes. Psychoanalysis is also the filter through which we can understand all social phenomena such as religion, culture, history, politics and economics. Freud believes that his theory explains why we hold certain beliefs, spend our money on certain things, work where we do and love or despise our governmental system. Psychoanalysis, which Freud believes is pure scientific method applied to psychological and social realities, provides a reliable mode of self-understanding and paves the way for the best life one can hope for.

In a general way, Freud understands life as a struggle to negotiate the demands of competing internal forces. On one side is the id (literally, "the it"), an impersonal, irrational drive that seeks pleasure. Freud speaks of it as a sexual impulse, but his concept of sexuality includes all our pleasure-seeking drives. The id is an asocial, selfish impulse present in all people from birth. Opposed to the id is the superego. The superego is first shaped by parental restrictions that limit our pleasure-seeking activities and later appears as our internal appropriation of social restrictions—laws, rules of etiquette and unwritten principles about what is appropriate and inappropriate in various circumstances.

Id and superego are in constant tension with each other. Our individualistic id craves what social values tell us we should not have, except in small doses and within severely restricted limits. Society imposes these limits on us because, without these boundaries, it tumbles into chaos. Caught between these constantly warring factions is a third aspect of our inner life, the ego, which has to negotiate between the other two impulses. The problem is that our thinking, conscious ego is a latecomer to the game. It develops well after the id and superego have been in full operation for some time, explaining why Freud traces mental problems back to early childhood.

This highly generalized overview of Freud's thought (which doesn't even touch on repression, the unconscious, dream analysis, stages of sexual development, the Oedipus complex, the Thanatos principle and numerous other key Freudian ideas) gives us a starting point to understand the psychoanalyst's goal. Individual mental problems and social trials frequently spring from imbalances between the individualistic desires of id and the social and relational restrictions imposed by the superego. The superego's demands cannot be ignored because social, political and economic life requires structure. However, too much attention to such realities squelches the pleasure and freedom we crave, and leads to a neurotic life. On the other side of the equation, psychosis occurs when one loses touch with social realities and rules. The pleasure attained in satisfying the id is lost by becoming a social outcast. Thus, the best life we can hope for, what counts as salvation in Freudian terms, is one that strikes an equilibrium between these warring internal forces. Finding this equilibrium becomes more difficult as society increases in complexity because complexity breeds pressure for conformity. Thus, Freud says, social pressure increasingly diverts our pleasure-seeking, sexually-oriented impulses into competitive pursuits such as athletic or economic activities that are mildly-satisfying to the id, but ultimately benefit society.

This diagnosis of contemporary society lends heightened urgency to Freud's quest to erase all traces of the supernatural from modern thought. He believes that God is an illusion that originates in our early childhood experiences with our fathers. On the one hand, a child sees the father as their protector in a terrifying world. On the other hand, the father represents the superego, a coercive power that constantly checks the child's pursuit of pleasure. Our experience with society shares this same ambiguity; we depend on others for security but also recognize that it comes at the cost of individualistic desires. Freud says that we eventually recognize that neither daddy nor society can guarantee the security we need. Thus, we create a bigger coercive power, God, from these external authorities. In short, he believes that God is an illusion we invent out of the recognition that forces in the universe could easily overwhelm our own finite power.

Those who rely on an illusory God are caught in a no-win situation. A nonexistent God provides no security against real threats and keeps us from confronting the actual realities of the universe in an adult manner. In other words, belief in God represents arrested development in which we cling to the dream that an infinite daddy will protect us from all that endangers us. Moreover, this illusion exacts a heavy price on our happiness because God is the ultimate expression of the superego.

Societies willingly adopt the idea of God because rules smooth the rough edges of social interaction. However, if people recognize that laws and social mores are simply arbitrary conventions, it will be difficult to justify punishing those who break the rules. Thus, society tells people that social rules reflect the will of God. If you disobey your parents or violate social customs or rules, you don't simply offend the sensibilities of your fellow citizens. You are in trouble with God, and trouble with God has eternal consequences. This view invalidates the demands of the id and strips away any hope of happiness. For Freud, then, religion leads away from mental health. The road back to a more complete life is to kill the God-illusion and adopt a scientific application of psychoanalysis to our individual and social problems.

ROGERS AND PERSON-CENTERED PSYCHOLOGY

Carl Rogers (1902-1987) is the first great theorist of person-centered psychology. In contrast to Freud's rather dark view of human nature, the center of Rogers's approach is a belief in the essential goodness of human nature. The obstacle to realizing this goodness arises from the conflict between what the individual wants to be and the expectations of others. In fact, the very name of this approach, *person-centered psychology* (sometimes referred to as client-centered or humanistic psychology), recognizes that the goals of the therapist may differ from the client's. Thus it attempts to avoid imposing the therapist's wishes, expectations or worldview on the client. Therapy is to be centered on the client's aspirations.

Rogers was raised in a conservative Christian household. He found its approach to enforcing conformity in behaviors and ideas to be coercive, and he rejected Christianity in early adulthood. However, Rogers also found the same coercive tactics at play in psychology. While not as blatant in their attempts to compel people to think or act in certain ways, Rogers says that therapists' assumptions and goals will determine how a patient's problems are defined and what ends should be pursued. In other words, psychological systems and methods are not value-neutral. They have embedded assumptions about what people should be and how they should attain that ideal. Rogers's alternative is that clients, not their psychologists, should determine and attain their own identity. His term for describing this process is "self-actualization." Implied in this is the idea that we have potentials that cry out for actualization. The psychologist's task is to function as a midwife who helps clients give birth to a unique, self-selected identity.

The desire for growth, for the actualization of our own identity, is hard-wired into each individual. The soil in which people grow is love, which makes it possible to choose our identity with the assurance that we will be accepted. When others accept us for who we are or want to become, what Rogers calls unconditional positive acceptance, we can then regard ourselves positively and without conditions. The hitch in the quest for self-actualization is that unconditional positive regard from others is a rare commodity. Those around us communicate, directly and indirectly, that their approval comes with strings attached. It is not just religion or psychologists who place conditions on their acceptance. Authorities from all directions attempt to actualize an ideal for our lives by their judgments. However, this ideal may be far from what we desire. As a result, rather than actively embracing who we are and growing in that identity, we *react* in guilt to attain the acceptance of those around us. When this happens, though, others do not really accept us. They accept a set of expectations about us that is different from who we really are.

In the light of this tension, the therapist's role is to offer the unconditional positive regard needed by persons for self-actualization. This cannot occur unless the therapist attains an empathic understanding of the client. Empathy means to "feel with" another person, to be able, as much as possible, to enter the client's aspirations and visualize what constitutes self-actualization for that person. For this to occur, the psychologist cannot approach therapy as the authority with all the problem-fixing answers. The need for a psychologist arises precisely because other authorities have imposed their expectations. Instead, a person-centered therapist avoids giving answers in the traditional sense, because such answers assume a one-size-fits-all world.

At the core of Rogers's approach is his belief that seeking answers about the nature of reality, whether human or nonhuman reality, is a fruitless endeavor. What we know of the world can be reduced to our experience. Moreover, that experience is unique to each individual. The experiences of a client will not be the same as those around him or her, and they will not match the experiences of the therapist. Therefore, the counselor is to become a partner who helps a client understand experiences and the feelings that arise from them, clarify obstacles toward positive self-regard and model unconditional acceptance so the client can unconditionally accept him- or herself. With self-acceptance comes the inner freedom to develop our potential and grow toward our goals.

SKINNER AND BEHAVIORISM

B. F. Skinner (1904-1990) diverges from Rogerian psychology in two significant ways. While Rogers seeks to heighten personal freedom from others' influence so clients can actualize their natural goodness, Skinner believes that both freedom and moral goodness are myths. In reality, Skinner says, our behaviors are caused by external or genetic conditions, not chosen. Freedom is an illusion. Moreover, because ethical action requires free choice, determined behaviors cannot be described in ethical terms.

Skinner's psychology is grounded in the convictions of scientific naturalism, which we examined in chapter six. Like naturalism, Skinner maintains that the universe is a closed system of physical entities operating in lawful ways. Human beings are no exception. However, while Skinner agrees in principle with scientific naturalists that our story can be told most accurately in the language of chemistry, biology and physics, such descriptions are practically impossible. To reduce even the simplest human behavior to its most fundamental atomic, chemical and neurological components to trace the causal chains would entangle us in staggering complexity. Fortunately, Skinner says, the social sciences provide a shortcut. Instead of tracing the biological elements of human action directly, social science can identify social influences that trigger the biological causes behind our behaviors. With this qualification in place, Skinner agrees with scientific naturalism that human activity is reducible to mechanical causes. Philosophy, religion, ethics and all other nonscientific perspectives thus lack explanatory power because they assume that human beings are free.

The deterministic nature of Skinner's worldview accounts for the name attached to his psychological approach—behaviorism. Strictly speaking, human beings do not *act*, since acting assumes freedom to choose from a range of options. Instead, we *behave* according to genetic and environmental conditions. We may think we are acting freely. In reality, however, our behaviors are determined by forces around and within us. This means that our traditional approach of punishing conduct considered deviant or evil is a form of cruelty, since the individual who behaves cannot do otherwise. At the same time, Skinner argues that many of the activities we have penalized are detrimental to our survival and well-being, so they should be eradicated. We just have to go about it in a scientific manner.

Skinner says that the behavioral sciences allow us to discover how we acquire both life-enhancing and life-threatening behaviors. Once the diagnosis is in place, what he calls operant learning (or operant conditioning) will allow us to encourage the former and eliminate the latter. Quite simply, Skinner says, both humans and nonhumans will modify their behaviors if they receive reinforcements from their surroundings that either encourage a new type of activity or discourage the old. The principle is the same whether we encourage a rat (indeed, many of Skinner's experiments used them) or a human with external stimuli such as food or a comfortable environment.

For behaviorism, the goal of psychology is to better understand how environmental influences shape behavior. Our future should be in the hands of social engineers who have a scientific grasp of the complex web of determining factors that surround us. As their understanding grows, we can modify the conditions in which we live and, as a result, we can program people to live happy, peaceful and prosperous lives.

Thus, while behaviorist therapies may be used to help individuals modify activities that harm themselves and others, the way to create a better future for humanity is a total reengineering of social structures under the behavioral sciences.

FAMILY SYSTEMS THERAPY

The first three approaches are not simply therapeutic methods. They are, instead, self-consciously distinct worldviews within themselves. Each argues that the only direct path to mental and social adjustment is attained within the tenets of its particular worldview. In contrast, "family systems" therapy is not built around any particular worldview and is flexible enough to accommodate a variety of different models of reality. Moreover, family systems therapy does not refer to a single psychological school with a particular individual at the forefront. Instead, it refers to a group of therapeutic methods with strong resemblances. The common thread in the family systems approach is a rejection of treatment regimens that focus on the individual alone. The problem with these individualistic counseling models was particularly evident for those who worked with troubled children and youth. Addressing the psychological problems of the individual rarely produced progress because clients would go directly from counseling sessions back into the family situations that were generally at the root of the child's problem.

Edwin Friedman traces "systems thinking" to the development of computers in the 1950s. With computers came both the need and ability to process vast amounts of information, and those who worked with computers discovered a need to think in new ways. A linear cause-and-effect type of thinking was insufficient because the components within a system operate, not as individual parts, but as a piece of the larger whole. Friedman states that "The components do not function according to their 'nature' but according to their position in the network."[2] Each component would operate differently in one system than it does in another system.

---

[2]Edwin H. Friedman, *Generation to Generation: Family Process in Church and Synagogue* (New York: Guilford, 1985), p. 15.

Many therapists saw a significant parallel within their field. Earlier approaches dealt with psychological problems by starting with theories about the nature of the patient. Those problems would then be addressed by dealing with elements within the individual patient's mind and life. To put it in different terms, these therapeutic approaches focused on the *intra*-subjective life of the client. However, "systems thinking" recognized that the same client would have very different ideas, experiences and perhaps a whole new set of problems if he or she lived within an entirely different social network. In almost every case, the social network exerting the most influence on an individual is the family. Therefore, family systems therapy takes a more *inter*-subjective approach, examining family interpersonal relationships to determine how those interactions create healthy or unhealthy people. As a result, family systems therapy determined that it is not enough to simply treat individuals. Problems can only be resolved if family interaction changes.

Behind this insight is the recognition that no one is born into a neutral situation. Families have histories, and these histories contain certain values, expectations, traditions and ways of communicating. Our actions and ideas are shaped by the reactions and ideas of those closest to us. We find our place within families by seeking ways to exercise dominance or deal with control by others. However, this process is like a chess game in which a single move changes the entire complexion of the game. Because families consist of a number of interconnected relationships, change within one member of the family changes the entire family interaction.

This helps us understand the limitations of individual therapy regimens. Family systems resist change. Even when the existing family structure is unhealthy, the various members have developed strategies for coping with the situation, and these strategies become habitual. Thus, family systems therapy attempts to help all family members become conscious of the web of relationships and how a client's progress is dependent on the family's openness to change.

POSITIVES

We noted above that three of the approaches we have summarized—psychoanalysis, person-centered therapy and behaviorism—can be categorized as worldviews. Moreover, all of them rely on pictures of reality that are at odds with a broad understanding of Christianity on key points. Nevertheless, these worldviews contain insights that are compatible with Christianity. In addition, even in places where the metaphysical model may be unacceptable, some of these approaches offer useful ideas for therapeutic methods and strategies. We want to acknowledge both below.

1. The integration of psychology with Christianity acknowledges what we already do. You don't have to be an expert in educational or developmental psychology to know that you don't put your second-grade Sunday school class in rows and give them a two-hour lecture. Seven-year-olds are just not wired to learn in that way. Similarly, as churches grow, usually the second or third pastoral person hired is a youth pastor. On one level, this doesn't make much sense because this individual addresses the spiritual needs of only a small percentage of a congregation for a short six- or seven-year span of their lives. Besides that, they don't add much to the offering plate. On another level, this move makes perfect sense. Adolescence is a pivotal period in spiritual formation and most people develop their foundational religious beliefs during this period, so it is logical to allocate resources in this way. Both cases provide snapshots of how we employ insights from psychology to the practice of education and ministry.

The reality is that every human activity, individual and corporate, has a psychological dimension, and understanding the psychological dynamics of any such activity provides insight. Countless studies show that the religious beliefs and practices of adults have significant correlations to parental attitudes about religion, peer loyalties, educational influences and any number of other factors. With such information, some conclude that religious beliefs therefore can be reduced to an explanation built on such psychological factors. The problem with this is that even if (and this is a big if) we could explain why a person holds certain religious beliefs, this still leaves open the question of whether the person's beliefs are true. Moreover, this form of reductionism is just as devastating for atheists, since their own disbelief can be just as strongly correlated to their psychological influences.

2. Psychology helps us remember that salvation, in its broadest sense, is a process. Christianity uses the term *salvation* in a couple of ways. Often we speak of justification, the point at which we move into a relationship of faith with God, as salvation. This is not improper. However, another legitimate use of the term is often overlooked. Salvation also refers to a process that involves justification but also includes the sanctifying process, in which we grow within our faith, as well as glorification, in which God completes the process in our resurrected life. Christianity can incorporate the insights of psychology in the middle phase of this journey because we all have a lot that needs to be healed and brought into sync with God's will even after justification. God's children drag a lot of psychologically debilitating baggage into their relationships with God and others. Therapy can be an important part of the social and psychological healing process.

3. Psychology reminds us of how closely we are connected to our past and our relationships. All of the psychological schools outlined above draw strong correlations between incidence of certain behaviors and a person's past. Moreover, they recognize that particular types of psychological conditions are more likely when various types of trauma, such as sexual abuse, neglect or the death of a parent, are part of an individual's history.

Recognition of the connections between mental well-being and our history and relationships is not new. This awareness is embedded in Scripture. It makes sense of why each believer is part of a "great cloud of witnesses" whose history starts with Adam and Eve and includes all of God's people, regardless of time and place. It helps us understand why Scripture describes God's church as a family or a fellowship. The fact that being a Christian incorporates an individual into a new history and a new realm of relationships does not invalidate other aspects of our histories and relationships. Instead, the point is to renew and redeem them, placing them in the broader context of God's redemptive work. Salvation by therapy's story is often that our histories and relationships determine the contours of our lives. Christianity strives to heal those relationships, but also points out that they are not the final word.

4. Christianity and psychology both seek healing and health. If we all had perfectly adjusted mental lives, it simply never would have occurred to us to create the therapeutic professions. We create out of need, and the pervasiveness of therapeutic professionals in our world reveals the extent of our psychological dysfunction and need. It also reveals the deeply ingrained human intuition that psychological disorders are intruders that should be expelled and replaced with health. As simplistic as it sounds, mental health is understood to be superior to psychological unhealthiness, and the mental health professions view restoration to psychological wholeness as a moral mandate.

Christianity shares the belief that wholeness is a mandate and that salvation calls for a restoration to health of every damaged and dysfunctional part. In fact, for many centuries, Christian theology has often referred to this process of salvation and restoration as *therapeuo* (Greek for therapy or healing). That which we ultimately seek healing for is sin, but sin (that for which we are directly responsible as well as aspects of sin where we are the heirs of its effects) has many manifestations. Some of those manifestations appear in the social and psychological dimensions of our lives. Thus, when psychological resources are viewed in the broader context of a salvation that encompasses every dimension of human existence, it is a partner with Christianity in its quest for wholeness.

5. Christianity and psychology both acknowledge that human flourishing requires love, acceptance and respect. It doesn't take a trained psychologist to know that we could shut down most of the counseling centers and mental health facilities if people received the love, acceptance and respect that all human beings deserve. I'm certainly not suggesting that this is the sole cause of the problems that mental health professions work with, but it is a major, if not *the* major causal factor.

One of the reasons we adamantly refuse to cast psychology itself as an enemy of Christianity is that the need for love, acceptance and respect is assumed throughout the Christian story. God's most fundamental attribute is love, and every duty God outlines for us can be summed up in our responsibility to love God and others. The Christian understanding of salvation is boiled down to God's acceptance of us, even though we are incapable of earning that acceptance. God's respect for human beings runs so deep that he does not override our wills, even when we make choices that are utterly destructive.

Our point here is that psychology's insight about our need for love and acceptance is not some new discovery. It is woven into the fabric of our existence by a Creator who molds us with the need for these. When psychology draws these insights under the umbrella of the Christian story, it is simply thinking God's thoughts after God. When psychological tools help individuals express and receive love, acceptance and respect in ways consistent with God's desire for us, it follows channels of reality designed by God.

POTENTIAL PROBLEMS IN SALVATION BY THERAPY

We might sum up the problems we deal with here under the heading of faulty assumptions about human nature. If psychology is concerned with human behavior (my apologies to pet psychologists), mental health professionals work from assumptions about human nature and freedom, our purpose, and a definition of the essential problem that stands between us and the best life possible. Where we find fault below generally reveals areas we believe some forms of psychology have erred in their assumptions about human nature.

1. Many psychological approaches assume a high level of determinism. We have seen above that some therapeutic approaches are deterministic; they believe that our actions and beliefs are caused by biological or environmental forces, not chosen. This deterministic tendency is generally linked to the adoption of natural scientific methods (and sometimes a naturalistic worldview) and the elimination of any qualitative distinction between human beings and animals. For example, Skinner places determinism at the center of his worldview and draws most of his conclusions about human psychology from his experiments with animals. Freud maintains more distinction between the human and animal realms, but still views our mental life as the product of early experiences. Family-systems therapy does not construct its position on naturalist assumptions, but some variations of this approach assume a "collectivist" view of persons in which the individual is simply the product of their family environments.

A Christian position requires that we maintain an important tension here. Christians cannot deny that our activities are conditioned to some degree (Christians will disagree about the extent of this influence) by our biology and social environment. At the same time, this influence is not so great that we cannot transcend these conditions. Without human freedom, it would be impossible to assign responsibility for our actions and we'd have no foundation for viewing therapy as anything but an advanced form of mechanics or animal training. In the absence of choice, psychological problems are reduced to syndromes that result from flaws in the machinery within or around us.

The tension between freedom and the reality of biological/social influence in our behaviors explains why we seek a middle ground between the extremes of what we have called salvation by therapy and the biblical counseling movement. The former often reduces our lives to an effect caused by factors totally beyond our control. The latter does not sufficiently recognize that psychology can provide tools and insights that enhance our freedom to overcome the pull of negative influences.

2. Psychology often works from a reductionistic understanding of human life. Many things in this world are improperly named. "Slumber party" comes to mind, since it seldom entails much actual slumbering. "Goal line" in football makes a little more sense though. An offensive coordinator does not randomly call plays, but chooses them intentionally as a means to get the ball past the *goal* line. Similarly, when therapeutic methods are employed, the method is not an end in itself, but a means to some further goal. Just as the goal of a football play is clearly defined by the nature of the game, the goal of therapy is determined by an understanding of human nature.

One of the fundamental problems with salvation by therapy is that it starts from inadequate and reductionistic concepts of human purpose. The naturalist assumptions of Freud and Skinner create significant problems in defining purpose. As we have seen in chapter six, any purpose we assign to a closed universe consisting of nothing but variously configured matter will be arbitrary. Moreover, even if Skinner's behaviorist psychology can lead to enhanced happiness and longer survival or even if Freud's psychoanalysis allows individuals to find a comfortable place within a broader social environment, these are not our highest aspirations if human existence is more than physical survival and smooth social interaction. Similarly, Rogerian therapy may provide a wide range of personal self-expression to clients. When this happens, however, it substitutes actualization of one's own *personality* with the development of *personhood* and simply becomes another form of individualism. Achieving peace and stability for a client within a family structure is an important therapeutic goal, but if family systems therapy defines this as the only goal, it makes the family unit the standard for goodness and wholeness.

Our point is simple. According to the assumptions of Freud, Rogers and Skinner concerning human nature, a spiritually empty and morally bankrupt person could be considered psychologically healthy and whole. This result is possible because they define human nature in a manner that eliminates the spiritual dimensions and reduces ethics to a collection of values. Survival, social well-being, family rapport and freedom of individual expression are all worthy goals, and to the extent that psychology can help us achieve these in healthy ways, it performs an important service. However, if psychology envisions these as *ultimate* goals, it has a reductionistic view of human nature that is incompatible with a Christian understanding of human purpose.

3. Salvation by therapy reduces the human problem to a psychological problem. Our concern about salvation by therapy's inadequate understanding of human nature leads naturally to concerns about its definition of the fundamental problem that we must overcome to attain our goal. When therapy views itself as the means to salvation, whatever stands between us and the best life possible is defined in exclusively psychological terms. As a result, the answers must also come from psychological resources.

Within a Christian perspective, the fundamental human problem is understood as alienation from God. Psychological resources are inadequate to overcome this problem directly. However, our estrangement from God results in broken relationships with others and ourselves. Since restoration of these relationships is also part of our salvation, the weapons in psychology's arsenal can offer assistance in this process. If finding equilibrium between competing psychological impulses, medication, family counseling or other tools available from psychology help resolve social or emotional obstacles to full health, Christians should make use of these resources. However, if we define our most essential flaw only in social or psychological terms, we will not draw on the resources necessary to repair the most basic problem of human existence.

4. Salvation by therapy's assumption of value-free psychology is a myth. In cases where psychology has viewed itself as an alternative to religion, part of the argument has been that, unlike religion, it does not work from unverifiable beliefs or impose arbitrary values on clients. Instead, it has represented itself as value-neutral and purely scientific in its orientation. The obvious problem is that the idea of approaching psychology (or science) from a totally objective view is itself value-laden; it devalues anything that is subjective or spiritual in nature. Perhaps the clearest example is Freud's proclamation that God is an infantile illusion that hinders our ability to deal with reality. Thus, it is the responsibility of the therapist to steer a client clear of such illusions. Skinner believes that life should be structured by social engineers, but who or what determines the values of these individuals? Both Freud and Skinner build their worldviews on foundations that are anything but value-neutral.

Even Rogers, who takes great pains not to impose the therapist's values on the client, fails to recognize that his psychological method is anything but value-neutral. What happens if a client who believes that self-actualization requires that one's identity conform to divinely established standards enters therapy with a Rogerian? If the counselor encourages that individual to bend their natural preferences to a divine authority, it violates person-centered therapy's core value of individual self-actualization. If one is told instead that they should seek only the positive self-regard apart from any perception of God's will, this imposes the therapist's values on the client, violating a central doctrine of Rogerian psychology.

No worldview is value-neutral. Values are deeply embedded in a worldview's understanding of human nature, the divine, what constitutes truth and a host of other foundational worldview questions. Salvation by therapy cannot proclaim superiority to other worldviews, including that offered by Christianity, by falsely representing itself as neutral and unbiased. It can only make its case by demonstrating that its convictions and beliefs are better.

CONCLUSION

In many ways, we are an utter mystery to ourselves. Why do we fall in love? Why do we persist in habits and behaviors that we know are harmful? How can the same person act in horrendously cruel ways toward some but be generous and loving toward others? Why, in our dreams, do we show up at the Wal-Mart corporate meeting totally naked, and we don't even own stock in the company?

The popularity of psychology arises precisely because thousands of questions like this arise naturally in our thoughts. Because these questions go to the core of our being, psychology appears to be a more likely candidate for answering life's ultimate questions than fields such as mathematics, chemistry or accounting. In other words, the breadth of psychology explains why many view it as a competitor to religion, and even an alternative religion. To bring us back to the beginning of the chapter, then, this helps us understand how the therapist has, for so many people, replaced the religious authority.

Therapy, especially under the supervision of a Christian counselor, can help us work through issues that keep us from loving God, others and ourselves in healthy ways. It can shed light on difficulties caused by chemical imbalances in one's body. It can teach families new and healthier ways of communicating. However, any good thing can cause harm if used improperly. Psychology cannot provide a standard of purpose and completeness that God has created us for both now and eternally. When it moves out from the umbrella of a Christian worldview and presents itself as an alternative that offers salvation under its own definitions, it overextends itself. By itself, psychology lacks the resources to lead us to a life that is "as good as it gets."

10

THE CONTOURS OF A CHRISTIAN WORLDVIEW

We have examined the basic components of eight lived worldviews that are competitors to Christianity. Our task now is to outline the basics of a Christian worldview. However, we will approach this task from a different angle than in other chapters. One reason for employing a different approach is that Christianity is not primarily a philosophical system that is reducible to a series of interconnected propositions. Instead, the foundation for a Christian worldview is more like a story about God's interaction with his creation, and we analyze stories differently than we would a set of propositions. Moreover, while propositional or intellectual systems tend to be static, stories are dynamic. God's story shares that characteristic. As it unfolds on the stage of history, new elements and events are anticipated, arise and are incorporated with the older aspects of the story in such a way that the parts only come into focus in the context of the whole.

Second, this story reveals certain ideas about God, ourselves and the world we inhabit, and these play a pivotal role in a Christian worldview.

However, gleaning the right ideas from God's story is not the primary goal. The primary intent is not so much to *know about* God as it is to *know* God. Knowing about only envisions a situation in which we have all our intellectual ducks in a row. Knowing goes deeper. It doesn't just change our minds; knowing changes us. As we said in chapter one, the goal of a Christian worldview is transformation, the rearrangement of our identity, convictions, ethics and actions.

In this chapter, we want to summarize a few central elements of a Christian worldview, review places where its beliefs differ from other worldviews in this book, and examine some implications of these convictions for different facets of our lives. In keeping with our assertion that a Christian worldview finds its origin in something like a story, we will not start out with a set of propositions as a means of getting at its foundational convictions. Instead, we will look at five major parts of the story—creation, Fall, covenant, incarnation and redemption—to see what sorts of convictions naturally fall out of the narrative.

GOD'S STORY IN FIVE ACTS

Act 1, scene 1: Creation. God's story opens dramatically. The first sentence of Scripture tells us that God created the heavens and the earth (Genesis 1:1), most certainly a big claim. The next line tells us that God takes what is chaotic and disorderly (Genesis 1:2) and gives it order and logic, perhaps a bigger claim than the first. In this ordering process, it is noteworthy that the phrase "and God saw that it was good" (Genesis 1:4, 10, 12, 18, 21, 25) appears after various phases of his creative activity. When the creative process is complete, this evaluation is intensified: "God saw all that he had made, and it was *very* good" (Genesis 1:31).

Several important ideas about God seem to follow from this. For example, God does not himself need to be created since he is there at the beginning of the story. The fact that an immense universe appears when he speaks indicates that this God is incredibly powerful. It is also strongly implied in this story that God does not just create stuff that takes up space in the universe, but bringing order to it all indicates that he also creates the rules by which the material realm operates.

Moreover, this story tells us several important things about the world. First, our universe has a beginning; it is not eternal. Second, God intends to create, so the world is not an accident or a fortuitous convergence of random events. Since it is a created entity, the universe is not independent from God or self-sustaining. God's ordering of creation indicates that, while regularities in the world might be *described* apart from consciousness of God as its Creator, they cannot be ultimately *explained* without reference to the God who designs these processes. Finally, because God keeps calling things "good" and "very good" as he creates, it is clear that Scripture does not view the material world itself as evil. Instead, creation is good; it is valued and loved by God.

Christianity's starting point stands in stark contrast with other worldviews covered in this book. None have this sort of creation as a foundational idea. Some, like consumerism, do not even ask the question of where everything originates. Others trace the foundations of their fundamental reality only as far back as the beginnings of "my tribe" (postmodern tribalism), my nation (nationalism) or my self (individualism). Scientific naturalism is the only other worldview in this book that seriously considers the universe's origin. However, it adamantly rejects a Christian understanding of creation. Instead, it assumes that the basic building materials of the universe and the laws that govern it are eternal. As we will see later, the absence of a creation account creates coherence problems for these worldviews.

Act 1, scene 2: The creation of humans. The creation story includes a second key scene: the creation of human beings. Humans are a unique part of creation. On the one hand, we are made from dust and return to dust (Genesis 3:19). Like every other created reality, we are temporary and changeable. On the other hand, Scripture describes humans, and humans only, as made in "the image of God" (Genesis 1:27). Most biblical scholars argue that "image of God" refers primarily to our task of representing God's interests within creation. Thus, humanity is "called by God actively to represent his kingdom in the entire range of human life, that is, in the very way we rule and subdue the earth."[1]

---

[1] J. Richard Middleton, "The Liberating Image: Interpreting the *Imago Dei* in Context," *Christian Scholar's Review* 24, no. 1 (1994): 24.

Our status as both creatures and the image of God defines the nature of our relationships. God himself enters into relationship with humans in a unique way. He converses with them, blesses them, puts them in charge of caring for the garden in which they live and sets a boundary on what actions they can legitimately choose. We are called to exercise dominion over other creatures, so our responsibilities within and to the rest of the created order are unique. However, because the humans are God's representatives, this dominion cannot be one in which creation is exploited. The garden and everything in it was good, but insufficient to fulfill another relational need that God put within Adam. After the creation of Adam, God recognized that "it is not good that the man should be alone" (Genesis 2:18 NRSV). So God creates another human, and eventually they make more humans.

Quite a bit of important information follows from this because our relational nature assumes and encompasses a wide range of intertwined dimensions of our existence. We can illustrate this in God's command to cultivate the garden (Genesis 2:15). The social facet of human existence is evident in that both people are called to work together in the garden, and how they fulfill this obligation has ethical importance. While God issues commands to other members of the creaturely community (e.g., Genesis 1:22), his directives to the humans have a unique feature because they are volitional beings and can choose to obey or disobey God's commands. We also find biological and economic dimensions in this task: Adam and Eve must cultivate the garden so it will provide the material goods necessary to sustain their bodies. Acknowledgment of their rational capacities runs just below the surface in the story. Unlike the other creatures in the garden, human beings lack an instinctual understanding of how to procure what they need for food, shelter and (later) clothing. Reason teaches them how to provide for their physical needs, among other things.

Our point is that God's story portrays humans as multidimensional beings. All these creaturely capacities result from God's creative activity and are part of how we are intended to interact with God, each other and the rest of creation. In short, this indicates that every dimension of life has spiritual significance. Adam and Eve's relationship with God cannot be separated from how they interact with what is placed under their management, nor can it be separated from their obedience to the limits God establishes. This also explains why we have found the other worldviews in this book inadequate. They absolutize a single facet of our being and are therefore reductionistic. Individualism, by absolutizing the individual, cannot adequately address our social nature. Moral relativism wants to absolutize our freedom and volition, but it ignores ethical limits on their legitimate expression. Postmodern tribalism undermines individual moral responsibility by making people the products of their culture. Scientific naturalism finds the intellectual realm incompatible with the divine and sacrifices the spiritual component of our lives.

The implications for how God creates us are vast, so we can only scratch the surface on this topic. However, as a general statement, this is the foundation for our recurring theme that every aspect of our lives must be drawn under the umbrella of our relationship with God. Psychological health, financial responsibility and productivity, loyalty to nation, a sense of cultural pride and an active prayer life are components of our existence and fall under our quest for salvation. To make a single facet of personality the sole focus of salvation leaves other vital parts of human life out of the process, and makes impossible the wholeness God intends for his creatures.

Also embedded in this part of God's story is the idea that creation is significant. God loves and cares for what he created by supplying all that humans need for a complete life. God gives them creative outlets in which all the capacities he has given them can be used in productive and satisfying ways. The humans are valuable to each other as social and work partners. The plants in the garden are valuable for supplying their aesthetic (they are told to enjoy the beauty of the garden) and biological needs. Thus, Adam and Eve are to care for each other and the garden in which they live. However, the ultimate reason for valuing creation is not its usefulness. Instead, the source of creation's value and significance is God's love for it.

Competing worldviews acknowledge also that we have an obligation to love others and care for creation. However, their foundation for these duties is shaky. The convictions of individualism, moral relativism, person-centered therapy and consumerism state that we should care for people and things, but only if they help me achieve personal ends. If they do not perform this function, they should be discarded. Naturalism in its various forms cannot explain either how humans can love or why we should love others. The beliefs of tribalism and nationalism prescribe love and care for insiders as a survival strategy, but view outsiders as a danger. In contrast, a Christian worldview says that all creation, human and nonhuman alike, becomes valuable, significant and lovable because God values and loves it.

In God's story, human significance comes with unique responsibilities. The God with the power to create universes out of nothing turns over certain powers to Adam and Eve. In a sense, God takes them on as partners and gives them management duties over a piece of his domain. Their task is to use all the capacities he has given them—working together, thinking, consuming and choosing—in ways that reflect God's love toward what ultimately belongs to him. The last point marks an important aspect of their responsibility. The humans have their place in God's world, and it has significance because God values it. But their place is not the same as God's place, so their duties come with limitations. Their capacities, their wills in particular, give them the possibility of overstepping their boundaries, and that sets up the next act in God's story.

Act 2: The Fall. A common feature of enduring stories is tragedy. Christianity is no different. Adam and Eve are given a great amount of freedom, but with one limitation: "You may freely eat of every tree of the garden; but of the tree of the knowledge of good and evil you shall not eat" (Genesis 2:16-17 nrsv). The tragic part of the Christian story is that the humans overstep this one boundary, and it messes up their lives. The problem for us is that this does not just disrupt the lives of Adam and Eve. The entire human race (with one exception) and every other part of creation gets tangled up in this disobedience and its awful aftereffects. This event is generally referred to as "the Fall" because creation's goodness gets twisted and distorted by it. Harmony becomes discord; peace degenerates into strife and death. This fall from goodness results in a corruption of a good creation that colors everything else in the remainder of the story.

Christians have disagreed for centuries about the mechanism by which all creation becomes implicated in this rebellion, but there is agreement about what is at the root of it—pride. As it is used in this context, pride refers to elevating ourselves to a position that properly belongs to God alone. The temptation for self-elevation is found in act 2 when the serpent tells Adam and Eve, "you will be like God" (Genesis 3:5) if you eat the forbidden fruit. The primary reality behind the Fall, then, is not that these first people eat something that is forbidden. The problem is that they want to be something they are not. They overstep their boundary and attempt to take what does not belong to them.

My ten-year-old son is bright, funny and talented. Nevertheless, I don't allow him to drive my pick-up, stay out until midnight or own a gun, and it will be several years before he gets a credit card. He is a great kid and right where a ten-year-old should be; but he's not an adult. Therefore, if he chooses to engage in these forbidden activities, the results will be harmful. Adam and Eve were created with freedoms and duties that were appropriate for humans. In fact, they were originally right where human beings were supposed to be. However, they were not (and could not be) God. When they overreach into God's turf, the results are disastrous.

This is the tragedy of pride. Though they cultivated the garden, ultimately Adam and Eve depended on God for everything that sustained their existence, and even for existence itself. This should have made them humble. Instead, they arrogantly grasped at the one thing not given to them. A reality check should have made them grateful for the power, responsibility and freedom God had given them. Instead, their lack of gratitude compelled them to seek even more. Everything the humans received as a result of God's loving creation should have caused them to reciprocate that love. Instead, pride twists this into a destructive self-love. In short, the Fall involves misuse of the good received from God.

Misuse of God's goods has consequences that shake the entire created realm from the moment it occurs up to the present. Thus, if the theme of the first act is that God has initiated a relationship with his creation, the second act in God's story is characterized by disruption of this relationship. Originally, the humans had open and honest communication with God. When God came to them after their disobedience, however, "the man and his wife hid themselves from the presence of the Lord God among the trees of the garden" (Genesis 3:8 NRSV). Their relationship with God goes from openness to hiding, and it does not stop there. When God asks how this comes about, the man shifts the blame to his wife (Genesis 3:12). The humans become alienated from each other. It spirals downward from there. Their son Cain murders his brother Abel in a jealous rage (Genesis 4:1-16). Lamech (Genesis 4:23-24) introduces clan vengeance and killing. Notice sin's progression. "A distorted relationship with God results in a damaged, fragmented couple, a damaged, fragmented family, and eventually a damaged, fragmented society."[2]

Every part of the story that follows the Fall exhibits the corrosive effects of our rebellion. It's not just there in the Bible, though. It permeates our lives. That is why, unlike the story of creation, every worldview has to address the question of sin and brokenness. Every philosopher and religion acknowledges that something is deeply and universally wrong with us. As Reinhold Niebuhr puts it, "The doctrine of original sin is the only empirically verifiable doctrine of the Christian faith."[3]

We feel this tragic wrongness in our bones and just cannot ignore it. That doesn't mean, however, that every worldview interprets this distortion of creation in the same way. When the New Age feels this wrongness, it interprets it as an imprisonment of our Divine Self by dualistic illusions. Nationalism defines our problem as military or economic insecurity. Naturalist worldviews argue that reliance on outmoded superstition creates problems that can only be cured by science. In sum, every worldview throughout history is profoundly aware that something is seriously wrong with us. However, the diagnoses differ radically.

One reason we can agree with substantial swaths of these various worldviews grows out of the Christian conviction that sin infects every

---

[2]Quotation from class lecture by Rev. Mike Platter, spring 2007.
[3]Reinhold Niebuhr, *Man's Nature and His Communities* (New York: Scribner, 1965), p. 24.

dimension of life. Thus, when New Agers are concerned about overemphasis on the material to the exclusion of spirituality or when nationalists worry about political or economic instability, Christians can be quick to offer qualified agreement. A Christian worldview should not waver in seeing these as problems. The difference is that God's story defines them, not as *the* problem, but as a symptom of a larger problem. This brings us back to the charge of reductionism. One reason the competing worldviews in this book fail is because they do not have a big enough view of the problem. Sin seeps out in every facet of life; it shows up everywhere. Thus, a healthy Christian worldview acknowledges the economic, social, moral, psychological, spiritual and intellectual dimensions of sin, without reducing it to any one area of our existence.

One basic motivation for this book is our conviction that the reductionism in competing worldviews represents a misdiagnosis of the fundamental problem of human existence. Moreover, we believe this misdiagnosis is connected with the downward spiral that follows the Fall. If the fundamental problem results from overextension of our claims into God's territory, attempting to resolve the problem by our own efforts simply perpetuates the problem. That is exactly what we find in each of these competing worldviews. Consumerism attempts to fix the problem by the accumulation of more money and stuff. Salvation by therapy puts the therapist in the God-slot. Though they get there in different ways, New Age and individualism both make each person the primary reality of their own universe. Nationalism and postmodern tribalism elevate some political or social structure to the position of ultimate authority. One of the basic worldview questions is, who gets to be God? Christianity insists that only God can fit this role, and that the primal sin is the replacement of God with anything less.

Like most tragedies, then, this tragic section of the Christian story has a hefty dose of ironic humor. After we have gotten ourselves into this mess by overextension into God's territory, we then come up with the brilliant idea that we can fix it on our own, which simply perpetuates the problem of pushing God out of the picture. We redefine the problem as the solution and put our trust in therapy, government programs, cultural isolation, money, education and other things.

The irony is that all of these solutions may indeed play a role in pushing back the horrific consequences of the Fall, but only if they find their proper place under God's dominion. However, they become just another part of the problem if we see them as *the* answer. If any one or combination of these "fixes" is not placed under God's authority, we simply perpetuate our disasters. Thus, from the perspective of a Christian worldview, attempts to dig ourselves out of the hole by our own efforts only mire us more deeply in the hole unless these efforts are brought under God's control. In an ironic sense, then, it is humorous that we insist on independence from God in seeking solutions for a Fall that resulted from declaring independence from God. Despite the humor of it all, it remains extremely tragic.

Act 3: The covenant. Most stories would be over at this point. A gracious God creates a good and beautiful world. Humanity spurns the goodness and grace of creation and rebels. You might think that God would be done with us, and for a while, it looks like that is the direction this story will take. God sees that sin is so pervasive in humanity "that every inclination of the thoughts of their hearts was only evil continually" (Genesis 6:5 NRSV) and says, "I will blot out from the earth the human beings I have created—people together with animals and creeping things and birds of the air, for I am sorry that I have made them" (Genesis 6:7 NRSV). Yet through this flood, God preserves Noah and his family, and makes an agreement, a covenant, with them. "I will never again curse the ground because of humankind, for the inclination of the human heart is evil from youth; nor will I ever again destroy every living creature as I have done" (Genesis 8:21 NRSV).

With this covenant, God takes the initiative to reestablish relationship with humanity, even though they do not deserve it. Under the most unlikely circumstances, he creates a people through Abraham and preserves them through equally unlikely circumstances. For example, they all end up as slaves under the most powerful empire of the day, and God brings them out and, after a very long journey, gives them a land. At times, this covenant group flourishes as a nation. At other points, it looks like they will be obliterated. They are devastated by conquest and carried into exile by Babylonia and Persia. After they are allowed to return to the land, they become a tiny piece in a Greek Empire, and later an even smaller piece of the Roman Empire.

Through all the ups and downs, God mercifully preserves his people. At various points, we see shining examples of faithfulness and gratitude toward this preservation. More often, however, God's people exhibit the same arrogance and forgetfulness that brought about the Fall. The point of this part of the story, which stretches over centuries, is not the faithfulness of God's people (although that is the ideal). Instead, it is God's faithfulness to his people. Even when they place their reliance on the tools other kingdoms use to gain power or when they ignore the pleas of God's prophets, God holds up his end of the covenant. This is the sort of grace that becomes intensified in the next two acts of the story.

Act 4: The incarnation. If our essential problem stems from declaring independence from God and attempting to usurp his role, the solution requires that we return to proper dependence on God. However, we seem incapable of doing that on our own. Our failure to hold up our end of the covenant reveals that time and time again. We need help. We need a savior, other than ourselves. This brings us to the fourth act of God's story—the incarnation. Incarnation refers to the belief that God became flesh in the person of Jesus. Without doubt, this is a challenging idea because we know all too well what human beings in their present condition are like. We also have some concept of what God is like. The tension arises, then, because the two do not seem to match in a way that can be easily understood.

It may be helpful to know that the early Christians had the same struggle. Their experience with Jesus confirmed to them that he was both human and God, but debates over how we put this together occupied the early Christians for several centuries. Perhaps it is best to view Christianity's understanding of the incarnation in terms of what it rejected. A group called the Ebionites believed that Jesus was just a very good person who was chosen by God to be the Messiah. This meant he was not fully divine. Others, the Docetists, believed that Jesus was really God but not fully human. His physical body was actually an illusion. The Nestorians suggested that in Jesus there were two separate natures. When he was doing miracles, his divine nature was active. When he cried or winced in pain, his human nature was expressed. In other words, the two natures were not united in Jesus but simply occupied different spaces within him. All three views were rejected by the church because, in one way or another, they did not fully express the conviction that complete divinity and complete humanity are completely unified in one person.

Traditionally Christianity has focused more on what the incarnation tells us about God and us, rather than on attempting to work out the technical aspects of this doctrine. Thus, the incarnation stands in continuity with the covenant of act 3, which stresses God's active involvement on our behalf. In his relationship with the human race, God makes a covenant with Abraham to create a nation from his offspring, sets his people free from bondage in Egypt, provides a homeland and sends prophets to guide and warn his people. The incarnation takes God's involvement to a new level. In the person of Jesus, God comes into our history and lives among us.

The incarnation also echoes the idea of creation by stressing the full humanity of Jesus. It is noteworthy that the Bible describes Jesus as "the image of God" (2 Corinthians 4:4), the same label given to the first humans (Genesis 1:26-27). This suggests that Jesus' humanity reflects God's intention for all of us—a life in perfect relationship with God. Jesus is not perfect because his humanity is obliterated. Instead, humanity is fulfilled in him. In Jesus, the material does not drag down the divine; rather, the divine elevates the created and the physical. If Jesus is fully human, his call to follow him and live as he lived means that we can no longer excuse our sin because we are human.

The difficulties in getting our minds around the incarnation can be traced to the second act of the story. Humanity has been in exile from the garden for so long that, without the incarnation, we have lost sight of a time when creation was not in rebellion to God. The Fall infects everything to such an extent that we cannot remember the peaceful unity of creation and the divine.

Thus, the current state of disharmony between creation and God tends to lead us in one of two directions. The first is a tendency toward a monism that absorbs one realm into the other. New Age thought devalues the material realm as a mere mirage, and its monism absorbs everything into the divine. Naturalism's monism goes the other direction. It eliminates the divine and reduces everything to the material. The second direction is a strong dualism that views the physical and the divine as incompatible. Unfortunately, this sort of dualism shows up most frequently in the place where it should never occur—in Christianity. Many Christians throughout history have viewed the physical as evil or a hindrance to spirituality. The idea is that, if we really want to connect with God, we need to ignore every dimension of our existence except our spiritual capacities.

This dualistic response falls prey to two mistakes. First, we have no unblemished spiritual part that can save us from sin. Every aspect of our being is implicated in the Fall. Thus, salvation must reach into every dimension of our lives. The second mistake is the failure to recognize that Jesus' humanity is robust and full-blooded. What is united with God in the incarnation is not a disembodied spiritual entity, but a physical, psychological, social, intellectual and spiritual human. Thus, it is not the physical that is inherently sinful. In the human race, the physical, along with all our other capacities, *becomes* sinful.

Therefore, the incarnation points beyond monism or oppositional dualism toward a third way of understanding the proper relationship between God and creation. The incarnation is dualistic in the sense that, in Jesus, God does not stop being God and the human Jesus does not cease to be human. However, the incarnation symbolizes the ideal of relational unity, a unity of will and love between God and his creation.

Act 1 informs us that God knows us because he created us. The incarnation reminds us, however, that this is not arm's-length knowledge. God also knows us from inside the humanity that he gave himself in Jesus. In Jesus' earthly life, he got hungry, enjoyed friends, experienced happiness and anger, got tired after a long journey and suffered intense pain. In short, he participated in the full human experience with all its temptations and challenges. The author of Hebrews writes: "For we do not have a high priest who is unable to sympathize with our weaknesses, but we have one who has been tempted in every way, just as we are—yet was without sin" (Hebrews 4:15). The last phrase highlights the decisive difference. Jesus' sinlessness reveals that, even though all other humans are sinful, humanity itself is not sinful. Instead, sin corrupts humanity. Thus, the fact that Jesus takes on real and full humanity demonstrates God's desire to save us *in and to* our humanness, not save us *from* our humanness. This brings us to the final act in God's story.

Act 5: Redemption. The last part of God's story is what we will call redemption. Scripture itself refers to redemption in a variety of ways, as we will see, but the basic idea is restoration. Something starts good, becomes corrupt and is restored to new condition. Thus, redemption starts from creation and draws all earlier parts of the story into its conclusion.

In the Christian story, the fifth act begins before the fourth act finishes. Jesus, the sinless, incarnate God-human, is executed by crucifixion. However, his death is not the end; God reverses it by resurrection. This event changes everything because with it comes the possibility that death and separation from God can be reversed for all creation. As with many other doctrines, Christians have differing formulations concerning the way in which the death and resurrection of Jesus restores our relationship with God. We will sidestep these discussions here because, in keeping with the nature of the story, participation in the redemption that Jesus brings is not dependent on a precise understanding of *how* he does it.

We stated above that Jesus' death and resurrection hold the *possibility* of redemption. We need to clear up one potential misunderstanding here, because the problem is not that God might or might not be able to pull it off. Instead, redemption remains a possibility because of us. God did not override the will of Adam and Eve in the garden, so they had the possibility of rebelling against God. Similarly, God does not override our wills when he offers us redemption. We can remain in a state of rebellion if we so choose. Our difficulty in taking up God's offer of redemption is that our participation in the Fall inclines us to remain alienated from God. Thus, as we have seen over and over in the story, God takes the initiative in restoring relationship. In this phase, God comes in the form of the Holy Spirit to allow our wills to be reunited with his and incorporates us into his covenant people.

The terms of this reunification is what Scripture calls faith. Faith is often defined as belief in certain ideas, but this definition stops short of its full Christian meaning. Faith encompasses both *what we believe* as well as *how we believe*. The latter refers to the commitment of our entire being, a trust in God to bring salvation. Intellectual assent to certain ideas is not enough. Faith in Jesus' redemptive work should touch and transform every aspect of life. God's story should rewrite our individual stories in such a way that our identities, convictions, values and actions are in sync with God's will.

While Christianity may be unique in referring to itself as a faith system, it is not unique in *being* a faith system. Every worldview is a faith system. Like Christianity, every worldview has beliefs that aim at reshaping our lives. Moreover, each worldview argues that something is profoundly wrong with the world and that its diagnosis of the problem provides the prescription for fixing what is wrong. Every worldview is also a faith system in that salvation is something in the future, something hoped for. The current fallen condition of the world means that the jury is still out on whether their prescriptions actually will bring the envisioned salvation. Given the messed up nature of this world, none of the worldviews in this book have proof that their salvation prescription will work. Instead, they have faith.

The question we must ask now is how Christianity's concept of redemption stacks up against those of other faith systems we have surveyed. While we have examined their concepts of salvation in earlier chapters, we summarize below what competing worldviews offer as their diagnoses of our fallen state and their pictures of a redeemed humanity.

Christians should have little problem with many features expressed by these visions of redemption. After all, each seeks healing for some aspect of life where sin's effects are felt. Indeed, we have argued that each of these components of human life is given legitimacy in creation and that each is in need of redemption. The problem is that each model of salvation above offers redemption only to a portion of life. They envision the individual in need of redemption as a spiritual self, an economic self, a political self, a psychological self, a cultural self, an individual self, a moral self *or* a rational self. Because their understanding of the person is partial, however, their plan of redemption fails to embrace all of life.

Table: Redemption Is . . .

New Age:	Liberating the Divine Self by overcoming dualistic illusion.
Naturalism:	Overcoming ignorance caused by superstition (religious and otherwise) and employing reason to solve all problems.
Salvation by therapy:	Becoming free to enter into healthy relationships with others and oneself by therapeutic means.
Individualism:	Using all available resources and freeing ourselves from all restrictive expectations of others to achieve our specific goals.
Consumerism:	Accumulating sufficient wealth to meet our needs.
Postmodern tribalism:	Overcoming oppression from dominating groups and securing cultural identity by political power.
Nationalism:	Preserving our national interests, traditions and borders by military, political and economic power.
Moral Relativism:	Freeing ourselves from the limiting value judgments imposed on us by others and tolerating behavioral differences.

In contrast, Christian salvation is described in a variety of ways, including as adoption into God's family, freedom from slavery, justification, forgiveness, being "in Christ," freedom from sin, new birth, new creation and restoration. These metaphors for salvation all envision a renewed relationship that frees us from all the distortions caused by sin and reunites the whole person with God. Thus, as we have stated earlier, redemption in Christianity is, in many ways, a return to the creation relationship. There is an important difference, as we will discuss below, because lingering effects from the Fall remain. However, at its core, redemption is about a reversal of the Fall, the return from exile and the restoration of harmony throughout the created order. Where sin had once alienated us from God and his creation, redemption brings us back into partnership with God.

There is much that could be said about the redeemed life; however, we will limit ourselves to two main points. One point, which we will develop below, is that our present state of redemption is real but partial. Salvation is accomplished from God's side, but our lives do not yet fully mirror that restoration. Our second point is that, if the root cause of the world's present state of brokenness and disorder is pride, redemption involves a reversal of pride. In short, acknowledging our need for a Savior means that we now understand the lunacy of putting ourselves in God's place. Moreover, since that Savior is fully God, allowing Jesus to save us means that we recognize God's rightful role, something we failed to do in the Fall.

Our acknowledgment of Jesus as Savior should be more than a verbal confession. Instead, it ought to result in total transformation. At this point, many think almost exclusively in terms of behavioral changes as indicators of redemption, and we don't want to overlook the valid role behavioral transformation plays. When our actions display a misuse of our God-given capacities, these actions should be replaced by others more consistent with our acceptance of his rule in our lives. However, this transformation should also go deeper. Thus, as we said above, pride gives rise to some ugly relatives like ingratitude, arrogance and an unhealthy self-love. Redemption should transform them to their healthy state so we are once again grateful, humble people whose primary love is directed toward the God who creates and brings us back into partnership with him and unity with God's people. In other words, redemption is not just about what we do but about the type of people we are.

As at creation, the conditions of this partnership outline our duties. We are to reflect the love that God has for his world in every part of our being. As God's church, his people, our task is to exemplify the character of God's redeeming activity in history. Thus, because God loved us even when we turned away from him, we are called to love those who hate us. Every facet of our lives—community involvement, work associations, friendships, family life, economic endeavors, even what and how we eat—should reflect an awareness that our redemption is a renewed call to tend God's garden. Jesus summed it up when he taught his disciples to pray that God's will be done "on earth as it is in heaven" (Matthew 6:10). Each part of our lives is to be oriented toward the goals and nature of God's kingdom. The obvious problem with this picture is that, at present, we do a very imperfect job of holding up our end of this partnership. As we put it in chapter one, our lives are often incongruent with what we claim to believe.

Reading God's Story Backwards

How does Christianity explain how it can claim that redemption has occurred and, at the same time, say that it is imperfectly (often far too imperfectly) manifested in our present lives? This question illuminates why we have insisted on presenting the Christian worldview as a story. Stories are cumulative. A story only hangs together if it pulls in the events of the earlier parts. Likewise, the last act in God's story continually refers us back to earlier acts.

The cumulative nature of stories means that they are messier than propositional systems. However, life does not really reflect that neatness of a collection of logically connected ideas. Life, redeemed life included, is messy. Christianity says that this is because act 2—the Fall—still exerts its pull. Thus, even among those who are mature in their renewed life, their actions, values and attitudes are still very imperfect reflections of God's ideal. While redemption has broken in and is a reality for those who have faith, the Fall still casts its shadow throughout creation. Sin's hold over us has been broken, but the effects of the Fall still permeate our lives.

If act 2 did not still remain a factor, if redemption immediately removed all effects of our rebellion, Christians would need no reminders that their faith can be hijacked by alien worldviews. However, under the conditions of the Fall, we still attempt to retain control of various aspects of our lives. Thus, when Christians fail to recognize that God is the owner of creation, their economic life remains in rebellion against God. As a result, many Christians try to worship both God and money. Similarly, nationalism can co-opt our faith to the extent that we think that God's work cannot proceed without our country's ideals or survival. In other words, we fail to recognize that our citizenship among God's people requires that we give our national citizenship secondary status. Quite unconsciously, we may so closely identify our "tribe's" traditions or practices with God's kingdom that we fall into cultural idolatry that fuses Christianity with tribalism. In short, under the conditions of the Fall, we continually face the temptation to displace God from different facets of our lives. More precisely, our present state of redemption inevitably involves displacement of God.

The good news is that, while the Fall still hinders the completion of redemption, it does not have the last word. Act 2 is followed by act 3, in which we see God's desire to reestablish relationship with his people. In act 4, Jesus' sinless life reveals the possibility of our own complete redemption. Jesus' resurrection is presented as a promise of our own, in which all the effects of sin are ultimately erased. Thus, we discover that we have not reached the end of act 5. Redemption remains incomplete. Covenant, incarnation and resurrection anticipate the climax of act 5 in which the Fall is completely reversed. Then, death will be "swallowed up in victory" (1 Corinthians 15:54) and God will be "all in all" (1 Corinthians 15:28).

But Is God's Story a True Story?

Our brief synopsis of the Christian story is obviously the "CliffsNotes" version. Much more can be said to fill out the details. Nevertheless, assuming we have given a reasonably accurate summary of the Christian story, we still need to address another important question. Is the story true? Does Christianity give an accurate account of reality, God, ethics, human nature, knowledge and everything else that should be encompassed within a worldview? While a defense of Christianity's central doctrines is not the primary intent of this text, we do want to make some preliminary statements about how to think about this issue.

A few Christians believe that a claim such as "God exists and is the Creator of the universe" is provable. However, most Christians would say that affirmation of God's existence is not subject to proof but is ultimately a faith statement. Describing such statements as faith claims makes Christianity suspect for many non-Christians because they assume that faith is opposed to reason. By this definition, then, faith is irrational and our choice about belief in God is purely arbitrary. The primary error with this understanding of faith is that it takes an unnecessary either-or position. It implies that a belief either is provable by reason or it is irrational. In contrast, our position argues that faith claims may not be provable, but we can make the case that they are not irrational. If this seems like a minimalist approach to supporting Christianity's core beliefs, it would be helpful to remember that no other worldview passes the proof test either. As we have shown throughout, every worldview is a faith system. We just happen to think that Christianity does a better job than competing worldviews at avoiding irrational conclusions and consequences.

We will use the question of God's existence as our first test case for illustrating what we mean. When we observe material objects which, by nature, undergo change, our experience tells us that these objects had a beginning. The universe is also material and changeable. Is it therefore irrational to believe that, if all individual material objects come into being at some point, the material universe itself had a Creator? Similarly, experience tells us that things like engines or synchronized stoplights, which display order and regularity, are designed to function in such a manner by a being with intellect. The universe has order and regularity but no human designer. Is it absurd then to believe that the laws of nature may have been established by a smart, divine architect? We also observe that every society has moral rules that it applies to human behavior, but they are not obligatory for ice cubes, snails, lug nuts or any other nonhuman entity. Instead, we assume that humans are the only earthly beings possessing moral capacities and obligations. It takes faith to believe that our universal moral sensibility arises because we are created by a personal and moral God. But given the universality of the moral impulse in the human species, this conclusion is hardly arbitrary.

In our opinion, none of this *proves* that Christianity is correct in its claim that God exists. Nevertheless, this seems more rational than the atheist's claim that the matter of which the universe consists is eternal, that irrational matter organizes itself according to rules (which also, for reasons that cannot be explained, seem to have no origin) that give regularity, consistency and predictability to the universe, and that some of this matter became configured into one particular species that developed moral impulses and capacities from components that are themselves impersonal and nonmoral. Regardless of whether one believes in a Creator God or in atheism, faith is required. This does not mean, however, that the choice between theism and atheism is arbitrary. Instead, our understanding of faith argues that we should choose to have faith in theism precisely because it involves far fewer logical problems than the alternative.

Another way of evaluating the faith claims of a worldview is to look for inner coherence. So how do other worldviews stack up against Christianity on this count? Our evaluation of this issue brings us back to two earlier observations. First, every worldview has an act 2 orientation. Each says, along with Christianity, that something is horribly wrong with us, and our experience seems to confirm that such a belief is, in itself, coherent. Second, every worldview envisions the potential of redemption; it holds out the promise of an act 5. The fact that every worldview holds out hope for redemption is another obvious indication that each and all are faith systems. No one has the audacity to claim that redemption has been realized and what ails every corner of life has been overcome. Instead, each non-Christian worldview has faith that its prescription will provide the cure, even if we do not see the fulfillment at this time. The question is whether this hope for salvation is coherent in the light of the affirmation that the world is presently corrupt.

The problem for Christianity's competitors is that they appear to have no precedent for hoping things can get better.[4] Without a creation account, their history knows only strife, warfare and death. Moreover, history is full of examples of those who have sought redemption by the various means proposed by these worldviews. People have long sought fulfillment in the accumulation of wealth and all that comes with it. What is the track record for this? The wealthiest in every age have always sought more or have come to realize that, even with vaults stuffed with money, something is missing in their lives. Why would we think that consumerism's future will be different? History gives us a long list

---

[4]It should be noted here that Christianity itself often does a poor job of recognizing the connection between creation and redemption. When the two are severed, many conclude that the fallenness of creation is so profound that its destruction, not its redemption, is God's final word for creation.

of those who sought to create heaven on earth by political means. Is it that we just haven't found the right political formula for redemption yet, or is it more likely that political, cultural or military programs are inherently incapable of producing the salvation we seek? We could ask similar questions about each one of Christianity's competitors, but what we are driving at should be clear. Throughout the history these world-views acknowledge, fallenness is the only word the world has known. Moreover, the historical record gives no reason to believe that future human efforts will change this situation. Thus, their hope that fallen-ness will not also be the final word seems incoherent.

We observed at the beginning of this chapter that Christianity is the only worldview in this text that includes a creation account. In a sense, we might say that creation gives Christianity more history than the other worldviews. This additional history becomes decisive in Christi-anity's claim to redemption because it takes us behind the Fall to a vi-sion of a world infused with goodness. Moreover, creation's original goodness is consistent with act 4's claim that Jesus' life exemplifies a perfected human existence. Both offer a precedent for redemption that shows that the current corrupted state of creation is not the only reality that history has known. Fallenness is not the only word in history.

Jesus' resurrection contributes an additional element: a Savior. In contrast with other worldviews examined here, Christianity acknowl-edges the failure of purely human efforts at salvation. If we want re-demption, it says, it will only come with God's help. Finally, the idea of a Savior is consistent with Christianity's persistent theme that God pursues us even in our state of rebellion. Again, while we are claiming that the Christian hope for redemption is coherent with other aspects of the Christian story, this does not prove that it is true. However, the coherence of the overall story, the inner consistency of its main ideas, should give us more reason to invest our faith in Christianity than in worldviews that lack coherence.

To conclude, we may not be able to determine whether the Christian story is true in the same way we could calculate the sum of a math problem, determine the weight of a goat or measure the distance from Earth to the sun. Such means of measurement work for certain problems, but they cannot resolve the question of whether Christianity, or any other worldview, is true. However, we are suggesting that there are other ways of deciding which worldview deserves our faith.

Our very brief and preliminary inquiry into Christianity's truthfulness has argued that our belief in a good God who creates us and offers us redemption is consistent with reason and experience. Without such a God, we are hard-pressed to explain how our universe came into being and manifests structure and logic, or why human beings have a sense of moral duty. Without such a God, it is difficult to understand why anyone would ever expect the world to improve. Instead, history should make us extremely pessimistic about our prospects for redemption. In short, even though Christianity's beliefs have their origins in Scripture, Scripture is not the only source we use to evaluate whether Christianity warrants our faith. Its teachings gain support from reason and experience (more about this in the next chapter). It still requires faith to believe the Christian story, but in view of the other options, it seems to be the most rational step to take.

11

DEVELOPING A CHRISTIAN WORLDVIEW

Our task is not complete yet, nor will it be in this life. Both in and between the lines in this book, we hope you have picked up on the idea that examining, evaluating and purifying our worldviews is an ongoing journey. Indeed, the authors' own continuing struggles to identify areas where our stories—our ideas, identities and lives—are out of sync with God's story is a major motivation behind this book. Many of the chapters have significant autobiographical elements just below the surface because we increasingly recognize places where we have bought into, and continue to buy into, stories like individualism, consumerism and the others we outline in this book (not to mention a few that are not covered here). Construction of our worldviews is a process. In fact, the belief that we have formulated *the* Christian worldview and have all the pieces nailed down flies in the face of a basic Christian premise that all human beings are finite and sinful.

Our assertion that fine-tuning a Christian worldview is always a work in progress is not to be taken as a slide into skepticism. The previous chapter should indicate this, because in it we identify the major landmarks of a Christian worldview. We are confident that our knowledge is sufficient to define the major features of a Christian worldview. Still, you may have noticed that we were honest about disagreements within the Christian community about how to understand the finer points of God's story. This is because we are also confident that our conclusions about specific connections, implications and details concerning our worldview should always remain open to refinement and correction.

This reluctance to attribute finality to any specific version of a Christian worldview, even our own, does not reflect distrust of God's revelation. Instead, our reluctance has two sources. First, it reflects our view that God's intent in revealing himself to us is to bring about our redemption, not to answer every intellectual question we might have. Second, we refuse to grant finality to any specific version of a Christian worldview because humans are imperfect and lack the ability to interpret this revelation perfectly.

The need for ongoing reflection on and testing of our worldviews brings us to our tasks in this final chapter. One bit of unfinished business is retrospective in nature; we will look back at what we have been doing and why we have been doing it. A second undertaking in this chapter will more reflective. Up to this point, we have employed a method in our worldview examination, but we have not yet reflected on the method itself. If worldview construction is a continuing process, recognition of the tools used in the project provides the means necessary for this process. The final part of this chapter is more prospective. It looks forward for answers to two questions: What should we expect from a Christian worldview, and how do we know that we are moving toward, rather than away from, the ideal represented by God's story?

RETROSPECTIVE: A LOOK BACK ON WHAT WE HAVE BEEN UP TO

This book began by noting that human minds are hard-wired for bringing order to the countless experiences, ideas and moral claims we encounter. *Worldview* is the shorthand term we have used to describe our efforts to fit these components into a more or less coherent system (although we may not be conscious at all of fitting things together). Thus, becoming conscious of this organizational process has been a major part of our task. At the level of consciousness, we recognize that these lived worldviews are answers to questions about ultimate reality, what human nature is like, how we know things, what is good and valuable, and what is necessary to squeeze the most out of life. This awareness sets the stage for evaluation.

As we evaluate the adequacy of competing worldviews, it soon becomes evident that not all of them give the same answers to life's most profound questions. In fact, some of the answers are polar opposites. In other cases, the answers may be the same, but different routes and reasons are employed to get to those answers. In yet other situations, we find variations between worldviews in what is emphasized and what is ignored as trivial or nonexistent. The bottom line, however, is that our lives will be shaped by the worldview that provides the steering mechanism. Different worldviews represent different ways of understanding the world, and they compete for our lives. Assuming our lives are important, the choice of a worldview must be viewed as a (if not *the*) central challenge in our existence.

Since worldviews are stories about how we live, the first part of each chapter has focused on *learning about* stories that differ from a Christian worldview. The central part of this has been a distillation of the fundamental convictions that define each worldview. From this, we discover how each worldview understands the world's reality, where it puts God in the system, what counts as truth, what is important for human beings to do and to avoid doing and what constitutes salvation. We have often used the question of human nature as a pivot point because worldview convictions determine which aspects of human nature will be emphasized (e.g., consumerism's emphasis on our material dimension) and which will be shoved into the background or simply defined out of existence (e.g., salvation by therapy's rejection of our spiritual nature).

Once we have outlined the ideas central to a worldview, we have asked what we can *learn from* each. Our evaluation of non-Christian worldviews has emphasized that they can remind us of important ideas that may have been filtered out of our worldview. They help identify blind spots or correct imbalances. For example, secular therapeutic approaches properly note that psychological and social healing is necessary for human wholeness, and psychology's tools often facilitate such healing. This brings a needed corrective when Christian approaches overlook this dimension of human existence. The New Age movement reminds us that God is not simply transcendent, but is also active in the world. Individualism rightly recognizes that God wants us to be successful in our personal endeavors, provided those endeavors are consistent with God's will. No worldview endures for long unless it contains a kernel of truth. To the extent that these non-Christian perspectives possess elements of truth, they serve the positive purpose of reminding us of ideas that rightly belong in a Christian worldview.

On the other side, we have also argued that these worldviews are competitors to Christianity precisely because they differ from God's story in fundamental ways. Thus, our evaluations have also focused on what we should *learn to avoid* in these systems of thought. Individualism does not give a sufficient account of our social nature, so whatever salvation it envisions must be gained by our own efforts. Nationalism, on the other hand, links individual well-being (i.e., salvation) so closely to a particular sociopolitical structure that an individual's fate is determined by the fate of his or her nation. Consumerism's primary story line is that security (i.e., salvation) is attained by accumulating physical goods. This reduces human existence to our animal life and ignores our spiritual dimension. In these and other cases, we have highlighted basic beliefs or assumptions of competing worldviews that are incompatible with Christianity.

REFLECTION: THE TOOLS OF WORLDVIEW CONSTRUCTION AND EVALUATION

Evaluation of our deepest convictions and the stories that shape our beliefs is of critical importance. Such an examination is not possible without a set of tools that allows us to be intentional about this process. Since worldview examination is an ongoing project, you will also need some of these evaluative instruments. After all, what we have presented in this book is only a sampling of worldviews. Others not covered in this book may represent a more significant challenge to your faith and, if history is any guide, the worldviews identified in this book will morph into new forms, and new worldviews will emerge as competitors for the Christian mind in the future. In light of this, we want to outline the tools we have used in our evaluative process in the hope that they will be useful in your own future reflection on worldviews. While some of these evaluative authorities should be fairly obvious from our own worldview evaluations, a couple of them operate more in the background and need more direct explanation.

The interpretive grid we have employed throughout goes by a number of names, but it is most commonly referred to as the Wesleyan Quadrilateral. Even though *Wesleyan* identifies this method with a particular theological tradition (that of John Wesley and his theological descendants), we believe that it is amenable to all Christian traditions since it has been used, in some way or another, by reflective Christians of all backgrounds. The *quadrilateral* refers to four resources for evaluating cultural stories—Scripture, reason, tradition and experience.

Before we look at each of these separately, we want to make three quick observations. The first is that these four sources should not be thought of as independent, but as intertwined authorities. Second, while the quadrilateral uses four criteria, not all carry equal authority. Scripture is the primary authority. The third observation is that, while Christians throughout history have employed reason, tradition and experience alongside Scripture to test ideas, Christians differ, sometimes significantly, on the appropriate level of trust we should invest in these authorities. Indeed, this is in the background of many ongoing debates within Christianity.

SCRIPTURE

The first and primary criterion of truth is Scripture. Thus, in our previous chapter, we relied on Scripture to provide the contours of God's story of creation, Fall, incarnation and redemption. It is the foundation of a Christian worldview. The Bible's narrative about God's involvement with his world provides trustworthy and foundational truths about human nature, about God's nature and about God's activity in our lives (both the present life and the afterlife). At the focal point of God's engagement with his creation, we find Jesus, God in full humanity, whose life, teachings, death and resurrection illuminate our understanding of God and ourselves.

While the Bible proclaims that God is the author of all truth, that he has revealed his truth and that his truth is knowable, it makes no claim to provide *exhaustive* truth. It will not tell you tomorrow's high and low temperatures, how to pick a lock on a bank vault or how to surgically repair a torn rotator cuff. Moreover, even its information on spiritual matters is incomplete, as we noted at several points in chapter ten. Details about the afterlife are certainly sketchy, and Scripture itself tells us that most of Jesus' activity and teaching is not contained within its pages (John 21:25). Nevertheless, a Christian worldview asserts that Scripture provides true and sufficient knowledge of God, his creation, our nature and purpose, and how we enter into and grow in our relationship to God. In short, Scripture is the first place we look and the final court of appeal in shaping a Christian worldview.

REASON

While Scripture provides unerring and sufficient truth in what it intends to teach, developing a Christian worldview requires use of our rational faculties as well. Though we could add to the list, we will mention three central functions of reason in constructing and evaluating worldviews. First, as we have said above, the Bible is silent on many matters. Its silence seems to indicate that it does not intend to operate as a textbook on organic gardening, art, physics, medieval European history and a host of other subjects. If a well-rounded Christian worldview needs to bring all reality under its scrutiny (and it does), our rational capacities must be employed to gather and analyze this information. Scripture certainly provides direction about how we should arrange and prioritize our information about such topics, but the information itself must come from other sources.

A second legitimate role for reason is the interpretation of Scripture. While the Bible is God's infallible Word, this Word must be read or heard. On the most basic level, reason must be operative for reading and hearing (if hearing means an understanding of what audible sounds signify) to occur. Reading and understanding do not take place without rationality. In addition, when we read and hear, we also interpret, which is a function of reason. We can't get around that. Thus, reason, the second criterion of truth, is necessary to help us properly interpret the Bible's message.

Not all interpretations of Scripture, or any other source of information for that matter, are equal. Some are better than others. Without getting into a full-fledged discussion of what distinguishes good interpretive principles from less adequate ones, it seems safe to say that our principles of interpretation must have consistency and must be congruent with the whole of Scripture. Consistency and congruency are two characteristics of rational thought. Thus, developing a rational means for interpreting Scripture is one of many necessary roles the mind fulfills in worldview development.

The final function of reason has, hopefully, been evident throughout this book. Reason allows us to organize and synthesize ideas into a coherent worldview. As part of this process, reason provides a way to understand how Christianity stands in relationship to worldviews that challenge and compete with the Christian perspective. There must be a commitment to reasonable integration that allows Christians to embrace what is true in different worldviews and the various academic disciplines, and to distinguish these truths from what is contrary to Christianity. Therefore, acquaintance with and analysis of ideas from different disciplines, cultures and worldviews are necessary to bring the Christian mind to maturity.

The need to rely on reason in worldview development illustrates why our worldviews are always fallible and incomplete. First, reason itself is fallible and incomplete. It is subject to the corrosive effects of sin. The second issue emerges from the first. Part of a Christian worldview is framing conclusions about how big a role our finite and fallen reason should play in shaping our understanding of God and God's creation. No responsible Christian argues that reason should be trusted as an infallible authority. Likewise, no responsible Christian argues that reason can be bypassed completely. Between these two extremes, Christians embrace a broad spectrum of positions on the proper role of reason within the life of faith. As a result, while the basic features of Christian worldviews may remain the same, the details of rationality's place within a Christian worldview have been contested for as long as Christianity has existed. The same is true for the relative role of our next two authorities—experience and tradition. All Christians rely on them, even if this reliance is not recognized or acknowledged, but in different ways and to different degrees.

EXPERIENCE

The quadrilateral's third criterion for sorting truth from error is experience. This term requires careful definition because *experience* is often equated with individual feelings. Many rely on such individual feelings as the primary criterion for determining whether something is true "for me." Because of the subjectivism implied in this, many Christians go to the opposite extreme and refuse to view experience as authoritative at all.

Our definition of experience is not subjectivistic. Instead, an idea passes the test of experience if its claims are consistent with facts, observations and actual life events. Thus, experience isn't pitted against Scripture or reason; the three are complementary. Life experience is one laboratory in which we test our understanding of Scripture and the conclusions we draw from reason. In other words, we are confident that the Bible's truth is consistent with activities that result in the well-being of ourselves and others.

We have employed the test of experience at several points in this book. For example, we have argued that it is impossible for a person to actually live as if no moral truth exists (moral relativism). Likewise, we have challenged individualism's assumption that each individual has sufficient resources to qualify the standard of goodness or the universe's ultimate reality. Both arguments are applications of the experiential criterion.

TRADITION

The final criterion of the Wesleyan Quadrilateral is tradition. Our use of *tradition* refers to the church's interpretation and application of Scripture to a variety of situations and issues over its two-thousand-year history. Tradition reminds us that our generation does not have a corner on truth. Instead, it tells us that we are connected with a "great cloud of witnesses" (Hebrews 12:1) whose collective wisdom can help us understand better how to navigate the Christian life. Even more than that, it expresses our confidence that, despite human limitations and sinfulness, the Holy Spirit works within God's people to preserve truth.

Tradition also helps us understand the means by which God's people have deepened and maintained their relationship with God. One such vehicle for transformation has been participation in authentic Christian community. From day one in the church, Christians were urged to meet regularly with one another for the purpose of spurring spiritual growth, speaking the truth in love, encouraging one another, confessing sins to each other and holding each other accountable. Christian community can be used by God to challenge us to take a deeper look at our convictional beliefs, especially when we can draw on the resources of Christians who are mature in their thinking and living.

THE INTEGRITY OF THE AUTHORITIES AND THE INTEGRITY OF OUR WORLDVIEW

As we have said above, Christians differ significantly on the role they assign to each aspect of the quadrilateral. However, of all the sources above, tradition might be the most contentious. On the one hand, the Orthodox and Roman Catholic strands of Christianity place great emphasis on the authority of church tradition. On the other hand, many Protestants view the overthrow of tradition's authority as one of the defining movements of the Reformation. In the light of this tension, we want to show that even Christians who claim to reject tradition's authority actually rely heavily on it. In outlining this, we will also be able to illustrate a point made above: these four criteria are intertwined rather than tests that are applied independently or sequentially.

Our primary source of authority, Scripture, did not simply drop from heaven fully complete as we have it today. To highlight just one aspect of Scripture's formation, it is clear that writings now included in our New

Testament circulated separately throughout the early church for some time. Along with these writings, other works were in circulation. Some were clearly Christian and were read as part of the early church's worship; other writings drew on Christian ideas and were even promoted as epistles and gospels of early church leaders, but were of questionable veracity. Our earliest list of the New Testament's twenty-seven books dates from A.D. 367, and this list was not made official until centuries later. To be sure, there was general agreement for quite some time about which writings had final authority, which ones were not canonical but still useful for Christians, and which ones were contrary to Christian teaching. The point here, however, is that agreement on which writings were to be considered Scripture is a function of tradition, the Holy Spirit working through and within the church. Thus, even those who claim to reject the authority of church tradition actually affirm it whenever they affirm the authority of Scripture, because church tradition is the means by which the boundaries of Scripture were determined.

The interrelationship of the four criteria in the quadrilateral is just below the surface in the three tests used by the early church to determine which writings were authoritative—apostolicity, catholicity and orthodoxy. Writings that came from those who were apostles, or close associates with apostles, were considered apostolic. In short, New Testament Scripture grows out of the tradition passed on by the apostles. The second test, catholicity (*catholic* here means universal), asks whether a particular writing was in widespread use throughout the church. Reliance on experience is evident in this, because universal acceptance within the church was seen as an indication that the writing produced beneficial results in the hearer's relationship with God. The final test, orthodoxy, draws on reason since, as we have stated above, rational thought is required to interpret Scripture, distinguish proper teaching from errant beliefs, draw out key doctrines and bring these doctrines into logical relationship to each other.

The interrelationship of the four criteria in the Wesleyan Quadrilateral helps explain our concern about reductionism. Throughout this book we have critiqued worldviews for reducing human nature to a single dimension. Postmodern tribalism recognizes the authority of various traditions, but absorbs our rationality and spirituality into them. Scientific naturalism does a good job of stressing the positive function of reason, but reduces our spiritual capacities to the category of superstition or subjective inclination. New Age puts all its eggs in the experiential basket, but allows no room for its veracity or authority to be checked by Scripture, reason or any form of tradition.

The benefit of the quadrilateral is that it recognizes the validity of all the dimensions of our lives. Tradition acknowledges the historical and social facets of human nature, reason recognizes that we are cognitive beings, and experience gives proper attention to our psychological and physical composition. Our argument, then, is that thoughtful Christians throughout the centuries have avoided reducing human existence to a single dimension by using the quadrilateral's resources. God has created us as multidimensional beings, and each aspect of our being has its proper use in worldview discernment and development. The goal of a Christian worldview is to integrate all of these God-given capacities into the service of God and others.

PROSPECTIVE: WHAT SHOULD WE EXPECT FROM A CHRISTIAN WORLDVIEW?

If you have invested this much time in a worldview book, it is reasonable to ask what we should expect from the energy expended in such an endeavor. Moreover, if the goal is to bring our worldview into conformity with God's story, how do we recognize when we are moving in the right direction? Adequate answers would require another book, so we will simply offer a couple of starting points for thinking about these questions.

In our previous chapter, we mentioned that redemption is a reversal from attributes that accompany pride, attributes such as arrogance, ingratitude and self-centered love. A Christian worldview should remind us of our multifaceted dependence on God's goodness, which should foster humility within us. Thus, humility is an important indicator of whether we are progressing toward conformity with God's story. The same could be said of becoming more loving toward God and others or living a life characterized by gratitude toward God. Both not only provide a partial answer to our first question—"What should we expect from a Christian worldview?"—they also address the second question—"What are the indicators that we are growing toward the ideal, represented by God's story?"

This may not be the type of answer one normally expects at the end of a worldview book. Instead of proposing a set of desirable virtues or dispositions, we suspect that many hope for a bulletproof system of Christian ideas that forces all competing systems into intellectual submission by sheer brilliance. However, we have argued that worldviews are *not just* systems of ideas organized by our minds, because human beings are *not just* rational beings. Therefore, a Christian worldview is *not* an infallible collection of propositions. There are two problematic elements in such an expectation. First, our worldview will never be error-free in this lifetime, because God alone has an absolute grasp of truth. We are not God, despite the New Age's assertions to the contrary. Our ideas, no matter how carefully considered, always fall short of perfection. The second problem with expecting our worldviews to avoid all intellectual errors is that worldviews are not exclusively about ideas. They are about what we believe about reality, how we respond to evil, how we assign value to work or play, our attitudes toward people who hate us, how we understand our identity, and what we do with our money. Worldviews, in other words, encompass the whole scope of our existence.

If our thesis that humility, love and gratitude represent major (but certainly not the only) goals and progress indicators of a Christian worldview sound too simple, let us point out two things. First, the convictions of most worldviews do not provide a foundation for developing such characteristics. If you find this difficult to believe, scan the worldviews in this book and ask whether their convictions support these attributes. Can you squeeze humility out of individualism, which puts me at the center of the universe? Does postmodern tribalism or nationalism demand that we love those who are not like us? Where would one find room in scientific naturalism or consumerism for gratitude toward God? The reality is that people guided by these worldviews do sometimes exhibit humility, charity and gratitude, but lack the intellectual convictions that make sense of such actions and attitudes. When this occurs, their worldviews are not fully integrated into every dimension of lives.

Unfortunately, this lack of integration cuts the other way as well. Thus, our second observation is that it is all too common to find Christians who possess the intellectual beliefs that should lead to lives marked by these attributes, but these operate only on the level of what we have called confessional beliefs. They know the right answers. They just don't live as if they do. These confessional beliefs never become true convictions that correspond to actions and attitudes such as gratitude, humility and love.

In both cases above, we are talking about failures of integrity. Integrity is frequently seen as synonymous to honesty, but Christianity demands a broader definition. Integrity is about integrating every God-given aspect of life—intellectual, volitional, social, psychological, economic, physical, political and spiritual—into a consistent whole. Integrity is when our confessional beliefs, convictions, morals, values, sense of identity and behaviors mesh into a seamless story that corresponds with God's story. This is what salvation is about. The quest to draw our worldview into closer conformity with God's ideal, then, involves more than getting our ideas right. As hard as that is, it is far too easy to confine worldviews to the realm of the mind. Arranging the intellectual pieces of a Christian worldview is child's play compared to living a Christian story. However, the focal point of a Christian worldview is not to develop abundant intellect (although the rewards of this should not be understated) but to live an abundant life. In the end, then, the effort invested in a worldview is aimed at experiencing the abundance God intends for each and every aspect of our lives.

Finding the Textbook You Need

The IVP Academic Textbook Selector
is an online tool for instantly finding the IVP books
suitable for over 250 courses across 24 disciplines.

---

ivpacademic.com